GO FOR GROWTH
by
PETER ANDERSON

CHRISTIAN FOCUS PUBLICATIONS

Published By
Christian Focus Publications Ltd
Geanies House, Fearn IV20 1TW
Ross-shire, Scotland, UK
Printed and bound in Great Britain

© 1991 Peter Anderson
ISBN 1 871676 70 3

CONTENTS

FOREWORD

It has been my pleasure to know Peter Anderson for more years than either of us cares to count, and I have always appreciated his straightforward, no-nonsense approach, which is well reflected in this book.

In these days of 'decisionism' and 'easy believism', when the currency of Christian conversion has been so grossly devalued, books like this are particularly valuable in helping young Christians to put on spiritual muscle, and I am happy to commend it for three reasons:

Firstly, it is *biblical*. You are not about to read Peter Anderson's opinions (though he has some good ones!) Instead, you will soon realise that as you go through the pages of this book you are being led through the principles of *the Book*. What more could you ask?

Secondly, it is *practical*. This is not a theological volume (which is not the same as saying it has no theology!). What it does is to take biblical principles and apply them to the everyday business of living in today's world, with all its pressures and hassles and hang-ups. No young Christian could fail to be helped by the chapters on Bible study and prayer, and there are excellent sections on many other subjects such as temptation and the right approach to public worship.

Thirdly, it is *personal*. Virtually the whole book is written in the second person singular; it is written to *you*, not some vague *they*, and I always find this helpful in a book of this kind. As an enthusiastic and competitive amateur golfer I have read shelves of instruction books on how to play the game, but I know that there is nothing to compare with having a professional at my side giving me a personal lesson. In these pages you have the best of both worlds. Here are sound and sensible directions, clearly and carefully laid down, with Peter Anderson as the 'old pro', gently nudging you forward step by step. Do what he says - and *go for growth!*

John Blanchard

1
YOU GROW WHEN YOU KNOW

The Christian life can be summed up in two words - decision and discipleship. Decision is the act of a moment, discipleship is the attitude of a lifetime.

Your decision for Christ, that act of a moment, was no doubt after a period of increasing awareness of spiritual need. First of all, you realised that you were a sinner and that you needed to have your sins forgiven. Secondly, you discovered that salvation could not be obtained on a 'do-it-yourself' basis but could only be found in the Lord Jesus Christ who died on the cross to save you from your sin. Thirdly, you trusted Christ as your Saviour. But behind the scenes, God in his sovereignty was at work in your heart and life. Jesus said, 'No- one can come to me unless the Father who sent me draws him' (John 6:44).

For some of you, that act of a moment cannot be so clearly defined. Possibly you could find it difficult to put your finger on a precise moment, or even a day, when you consciously trusted Jesus Christ as your Saviour. Do not worry if you cannot pinpoint the precise moment - what is important is that you can look back and say, 'Yes, there was a time when I did not believe in Christ, and had no conscious need to be saved and experience God's forgiveness. Now things have changed, and I believe, and I am trusting Jesus Christ as my Saviour.'

It is far more important to know that you are born again, than to know when that happened. After all, the new birth is a mystery because it is the work of the Holy Spirit. Possibly God will let you look at your spiritual birth certificate when you get to heaven!

To be saved is one thing: to feel sure that you are saved is quite another. Sad to say there are some who are true believers, real Christians, and yet they never seem to enjoy a complete assurance of acceptance by God. Their sense of sin is so strong and overpowering that they never feel confident that Christ has really accepted them and saved them. Those of you who are familiar with John Bunyan's *Pilgrim's Progress* will remember that in Part II, 'Despondency' and 'Much-Afraid' also arrived safely at the Celestial City as well as 'Valiant for Truth'!

A full assurance of hope is not necessary for salvation, and the absence of it is no argument against a man or woman's perseverance to the end, but a lack of assurance will certainly hinder your spiritual growth as a Christian. You will only start to grow when you know.

How can you be sure?

You can be sure first of all because of the *promises* of God contained in the Bible. If Christian assurance had your feelings as its foundation initially, then it would be a very insecure and unstable experience. Assurance would be subject to the ebb and flow of your emotions, to your physical condition, to moments of stress, temptation, and a thousand and one outside sources. No, the foundation of Christian assurance is the unchanging Word of God. The Lord Jesus said, 'Heaven and earth will pass away, but my words will never pass away' (Matt 24:35). Paul, the great apostle, writing of the Word of God and its relationship to faith, and then subsequently to our assurance of faith said, 'Faith comes from hearing the message, and the message is heard through the word of Christ' (Rom.10:17).

It was through the hearing of the Word of God that you were brought to an awareness of the fact that you were a sinner. God's Word pierced deep into your heart and made you feel uncomfortable. The Holy Spirit through the Word of God convicted you of your sin and showed you the Lord

Jesus as the only Saviour of sinners. Now, it is this same Word of God that says that if you have repented of your sin and are trusting Christ alone as Saviour, then you are saved: you are a Christian.

In the Gospel of Luke there is a story of a sinful woman who found forgiveness. Jesus said to her, 'Your sins are forgiven... Your faith has saved you; go in peace'(7:36-50). And all of this happened in the house of a self-righteous Pharisee named Simon. If this woman had based her assurance of forgiveness and acceptance on the attitude and words of the people around her she would have had very little assurance. Most of the guests would have shunned her because she was an obvious sinner. Certainly Simon the Pharisee criticised her to Jesus. If you had met her in the street two weeks later and asked her how did she know that she was forgiven and saved, she could only have answered, 'Jesus said so'. And this living Word of God 'says so' time and time again.

Listen to what John says:

He came to that which was his own, but his own did not receive him. Yet to all who received him, to those who believed in his name, he gave the right to become children of God (John 1: 11,12).

I write these things to you who believe in the name of the Son of God so that you may know that you have eternal life (1 John 5:13).

So the question is: have you received Jesus Christ? Are you among those who have trusted him and called upon him for salvation and forgiveness? If you have, then trust and believe what his Word says about you: You have eternal life. But here are another two promises of the Lord Jesus:

I tell you the truth, whoever hears my word and believes him who sent me has eternal life and will not be condemned; he has crossed over from death to life (John 5:24).

My sheep listen to my voice; I know them, and they follow me. I give them eternal life, and they shall never perish; no-one can snatch them out of my hand. My Father, who has given them to me, is greater than all; no-one can snatch them out of my Father's hand. I and the Father are one (John 10:27-29).

Have you heard the words of Jesus and believed? Then the promises of the Lord Jesus are for you.

Paul wrote to the young Thessalonian Christians:

11

May God himself, the God of peace, sanctify you through and through. May your whole spirit, soul and body be kept blameless at the coming of our Lord Jesus Christ. The one who calls you is faithful and he will do it (1Thess. 5:23,24).

Similarly Peter reminds suffering Christians that they are being kept by God when he says they are 'shielded by God's power until the coming of the salvation that is ready to be revealed in the last time' (1 Peter 1:5). Jude in his book of the Bible makes this point very clearly, describing the Lord as 'him who is able to keep you from falling and to present you before his glorious presence without fault and with great joy' (Jude 24). So here are just some of the promises of God revealed in the Bible concerning salvation - your salvation if you are trusting in the Lord Jesus Christ. God's salvation is a free gift, received by faith alone, and on the basis of God's grace revealed in Jesus Christ.

Augustine said, 'To be assured of our salvation is no arrogant stoutness, it is not presumption, it is God's promise.' Assurance is yours because of the promises of God and those promises are recorded in the Bible. Martin Luther sought for many years to find an assurance of his acceptance with God. When he finally enjoyed this assurance he wrote a beautiful hymn that clearly expresses the point:

> For feelings come and feelings go,
> And feelings are deceiving.
> My warrant is the Word of God,
> Naught else is worth believing.
>
> Though all my heart should feel condemned,
> For want of some sweet token,
> There is one greater than my heart,
> Whose Word cannot be broken.
>
> I'll trust in God's unchanging Word,
> Till soul and body sever;
> For, though all things shall pass away,
> His Word shall stand for ever.

Can I encourage you by saying that there is not one single example in the whole of Scripture of any of God's children ending in hell.

Yes, we do read about Judas Iscariot who betrayed the Saviour, and Ananias and Sapphira who lied to the Holy Spirit, and also Demas who forsook Paul. Jesus did speak about fruitless branches, and stony and thorny ground hearers. He certainly spoke about virgins with no oil in their lamps and servants who buried their talents in the ground. He was scathing in his comments about false prophets and hypocrites. He condemned their hollow characters and spoke of their destiny. But there is not one mention in the Bible of any believer falling from grace and missing out on salvation and heaven at the end.

Of course, there have been servants of God who have stumbled and fallen from time to time, and some very badly, but none have perished, none have been excluded from heaven. Does it not seem strange to you that if there was any possibility of a child of God ever being cast away from God's presence, that nowhere in the Bible do we have any example of it? There is none, because there are none, nor will there ever be such a situation. You can be sure of God's salvation and forgiveness because of the *promises* of God in the Bible.

You can also be sure that you are saved because of the *power* of God demonstrated in a changed disposition. Real faith in Christ produces changes in a person's life that can be seen.

It has been said that John wrote his Gospel to lead men to faith in Christ (John 20:31): and then wrote his first Letter to those who had come to faith, in order that they might have assurance of faith (1 John 5:13). He pointed to the indications of new life in a changed disposition, having different priorities and different desires. In his first letter, in chapter 2: 3, John writes about what we know: 'We *know* that we have come to *know* him if we obey his commands.' The word, *know,* occurs twice in this verse. In both cases it implies no mere acquaintance with, or awareness of, an idea or an individual. Rather, it indicates a knowledge gleaned and retained through personal experience.

The use of the tense is also important in understanding how we have come by this knowledge. The second occurrence here of the word 'know' suggests by its tense that the readers have come to know Jesus in the past, and so have previously entered into the family of God, once and for all. In contrast, the first 'know' indicates by its tense a continuing and ever-growing relationship; something ongoing and maturing. It might read: 'We continually and increasingly know that we have already come to know him personally if we obey his commands.' Christian assurance, therefore, grows as we grow in our Christian lives.

Now what are some of the things that can be seen in our lives that should lead us to 'know that we have come to know him'? What are these new priorities and desires? Notice John says: 'We know that we have come to know him *if we obey his commands.*'

As with the use of the word 'know', this word

'obey' is a very important one, and certainly it would be a very frightening word if it meant that we could only be sure that we were saved if we were able to obey every commandment all of the time. No, this word 'obey' expresses rather the idea of watchful, observant obedience. It means that we are to observe God's commandments carefully and consistently. Just as a child in a good family relationship obeys his parents out of respect and love, so a person who is truly born of God's Spirit wants to 'obey' his commandments. Lord Nelson said to a young officer, 'You must always implicitly obey orders without attempting to form any opinion of your own respecting their propriety.' Do you have such a spirit of obedience in your life as far as God's commandments are concerned? Obedience to God is a sign of a growing relationship with him. No experience that we may claim to have is valid unless it has moral consequences. John affirms: 'The man who says, "I know him," but does not do what he commands is a liar, and the truth is not in him' (1 John 2 : 4).

True love for God does not consist of words expressed in sentimental language, but in obedience to his Word: 'But if anyone obeys his Word, God's love is truly made complete in him. This is how we know we are in him' (1 John 2:5).

The desire to obey him is a characteristic of the one who has really come to faith in Jesus Christ. John says:

> Whoever loves his brother lives in the light, and there is nothing in him to make him stumble. But whoever hates his brother is in the darkness... he does not know where he is going, because the darkness has blinded him' (1 John 2:10,11).

Here John goes back to what he was talking about earlier: 'If we walk in the light, as he is in the light, we have fellowship with one another, and the blood of Jesus, his Son, purifies us from all sin' (1 John 1:7). True love for other Christians is the practical application of walking in the light. If you are really in God's family and living in fellowship with Christ, then you will love the other members of his family.

But I want also to consider what John wrote in 1 John 2:15: 'Do not love the world or anything in the world. If anyone loves the world, the love of the Father is not in him'. I will return later, in chapter six, to this topic of worldliness but it deserves mention here as our attitude to the world is closely bound up with our assurance of Christ's role in our lives.

This phrase, *the world,* can be difficult to understand because it defies exact definition. The reason for this is that it does not refer to something concrete or solid but is abstract. The *world* is, in fact, a spirit. The closest working definition I have found is that of Susannah Wesley who said, 'Whatever cools my affection towards Christ is the world.'

This is clearly a personal explanation and demands self-examination of the Christian's heart. There are, however, certain choices to be made which are clearly antagonistic to one another and these can be helpful in defining the *world* for us: belief and unbelief; righteousness and unrighteousness; light and darkness; Christ and Satan; the temple of God and idols. You cannot go over to the camp of unbelief without whittling down your belief. You cannot go into the darkness without leaving the light. You cannot serve Satan without denying Christ.

Therefore the exhortation is clear - make a clean break with all that belongs to the enemies of your Saviour. Anything that dims your vision of Christ, or takes away your taste for Bible Study, or cramps your prayer life, or makes Christian work more difficult, is wrong and as a Christian you should turn away from it.

There was a Scotsman who had a dress shirt

which he wore on special occasions. After he had used it, he would question its cleanness and take it to the window for better light. His wife's words were very wise, 'If it's doubtful, it's dirty.' As a Christian that should be your yardstick. Always give God the benefit of the doubt.

In Romans 12:2 Paul says, 'Do not conform any longer to the pattern of this world...' What he means is that because as a Christian you are different from non-Christians it should show in a positive way. The most positive testimony that you can have to a changed life is that you are not conformed to the world because you have experiencing the transformation Paul points to in this passage.

It is not a question of separation in terms of lack of contact with the world, but rather a question of separation in terms of non-conformity or non-complicity with the world's standards, habits and ambitions which are contrary to God's Word. James certainly spells this message out very clearly when he says, 'Friendship with the world is hatred towards God. Anyone who chooses to be a friend of the world becomes an enemy of God' (James 4:4).

Non-conformity to the world is extremely relevant to our personal assurance. Personal assurance is the privilege of every true believer. Have you obeyed God's Word in repenting of your sin and trusting Jesus Christ as your Saviour? Do you believe God's Word in what it says of you in terms of Christ saving you and God receiving you? Then there should be in your life something to show in terms of a desire to keep his commandments; to love your fellow Christians; and to separate from a world that hates you and won't submit to your Saviour.

Samuel Rutherford said, 'Believe God's Word more than you believe your own feelings and experiences. Your rock is Christ. It is not the rock that ebbs and flows - but the sea.' For you will start to grow as a Christian when you *know* and are sure that you really are a Christian. Growth will begin to show in a changed disposition.

You can be further convinced that you are saved because of the *personal* witness of the Holy Spirit in your heart. A witness is one who bears testimony or supplies evidence for the purpose of adducing proof, and this the Holy Spirit does in the heart of a true believer. He first of all bears witness to Christ, as to who he is - the Son of God and Saviour of the world. He then bears witness to the acceptance by God of the one who has come to Christ.

The evidence on which a Christian has the right to conclude that he is a child of God is not his own state or condition, but rather the promise of God in his Word and then the still small voice within that whispers - 'Accepted.'

Maybe you do sometimes feel tempted to question the Holy Spirit's presence within you when your heart feels cold and listless. But the fact that you feel concerned and burdened about it is of itself evidence of spiritual life. A negative way of claiming a positive truth but no less true because of that! If your desires are Godward, if you want to please him, if you desire to be like Christ, if you mourn over your failures, then far from being presumptuous to conclude that you are one of God's children, it would be wilful blindness to refuse to recognise the work of the Spirit in your life. Does your conscience bear witness to the fact that you honestly and sincerely desire to walk with God and to please him? Then God has 'begun a good work in you.'

Let's look at a remarkable statement by Paul:

For you did not receive a spirit that makes you a slave again to fear, but you received the Spirit of sonship. And by him we cry, 'Abba, Father.' The Spirit himself testifies with our spirit that we are God's children (Rom.8:15,16).

Here is the indescribable yet keenly felt whisper

of God to our hearts by his Holy Spirit that we are his children. Do you have this witness within your heart? For you will make real progress as a Christian when you really know for sure that you are a Christian.

You can be sure because of the *promises* of God in his Word. You can be sure because of the *power* of God in your life that is changing you. You can be sure because of the *personal* witness of the Holy Spirit within you.

2
YOU ARE WHAT YOU EAT

Bible reading is the number one priority for spiritual growth. Reading a book about the Bible can be helpful, but it can never be a substitute for your own personal reading of God's Word. Just as you came to believe in Jesus Christ through the hearing of God's Word, so it is that your faith will continue to grow through the reading and study of the same Word. The Bible 'will always be' a new book to those best acquainted with it.

Many things in the Bible are hard to understand. Yet, there is much in the Bible that we cannot misunderstand, and that is why even as a young Christian you can read the Bible and profit from it immensely. The apostle Peter says, 'Like newborn babies, crave pure spiritual milk, so that by it you may grow up in your salvation' (1 Peter 2:2). The Bible and Christian growth go hand in hand. But before we look at various methods of tackling Bible reading and study, I think that it might be useful to have a general picture of the content of the Bible.

The Bible is in two main sections, the Old and

New Testament, together comprising sixty-six books. Three groups of writings make up the Old Testament, and these are spoken of by Jesus as 'the Law of Moses, the Prophets and the Psalms' (Luke 24:44). The Law consists of the first five books, normally referred to as the Pentateuch. These five books are historical and give us a foundation for much that will follow. The books of the Prophets give us the action as they thunder out 'this is what the Lord says' to kings and nations. The other section, known as the Psalms, really recounts the experiences and feelings of man as he works out God's truth in day by day living.

When you turn to the New Testament you find four sections. First of all come the Gospels, which give us the historically recorded life of Christ, his birth, teaching, death and resurrection. The Gospels are followed by the Acts of the Apostles, giving an outline of the beginnings of the Christian Church and its rapid growth throughout the Roman Empire. After the Acts you will discover what are called the Epistles (letters), and these give an explanation of our Christian faith - what it means to be a Christian and how we should live the Christian life. The fourth section is comprised of one book - Revelation - and this tells us about the end of the age, the second coming of Christ and the final triumph of his kingdom.

It has been rightly said *that the New is in the Old concealed, and the Old is in the New revealed.* This is indeed true, because you cannot do without the Old or the New Testament if you want to get to know the complete message of the Bible. Whatever your taste in reading may be, you will find it catered for in the pages of the Bible, ranging through such various subjects as history, adventure, romance, public health, poetry, mystery and even law.

The Lord Jesus gave us the central message of the Bible when he said, 'You diligently study the Scriptures because you think that by them you possess eternal life. These are the Scriptures that testify about me' (John 5:39). The message of the Bible is Jesus Christ, so wherever you turn to in the Bible you can discover something about your Lord Jesus Christ.

Jesus repeatedly stressed this fact, adding that, 'If you believed Moses, you would believe me, for he wrote about me' (John 5:46). Later he said, 'Abraham rejoiced at the thought of seeing my day; he saw it and was glad' (John 8:56). Once in the synagogue in Nazareth, 'the scroll of the prophet Isaiah was handed to him. Unrolling it, he found the place where it is written: "The Spirit of the Lord is on me, because he has anointed me to preach good news to the poor.

He has sent me to proclaim freedom for the prisoners and recovery of sight for the blind, to release the oppressed, to proclaim the year of the Lord's favour ..." And he said to them, "Today this Scripture is fulfilled in your hearing"' (Luke 4:17-19,21). On another occasion, 'beginning with Moses and all the Prophets, he explained to them what was said in all the Scriptures concerning himself' (Luke 24:27).

These and many other Scriptures indicate that above all else the Bible is a revelation and declaration of Jesus Christ. Read and study your Bible and you will discover Jesus.

Trusting God's Word, the Bible

But the Bible is not only very readable, it is also most reliable. God's Word can be trusted for a number of reasons.

It is reliable, firstly, because of its remarkable prophecies. There are over 300 of these listed in the Old Testament that were literally fulfilled in the life of Christ. It is a statistical impossibility for Jesus to have fulfilled these by chance.

In addition, although the Bible is not a scientific treatise, it has remarkable scientific foreknowledge. Most statements in the Bible are twenty to thirty centuries old, and yet the Bible is free from the glaring errors of its contemporaries. Like

Aristotle, Moses had no instruments, yet centuries before Aristotle's discoveries about the sun and the moon, Moses wrote that 'God made two great lights - the greater light to govern the day and the lesser light to govern the night' (Gen 1:16). Notice that Moses did not say that the sun was the greatest light: there are stars far greater than the sun, but they do not rule the day.

The Bible's reliability can also be seen in that once upon a time, and not so long ago, science said that there were 1,056 stars. But thousands of years ago the Bible stated the words, 'I will make the descendants of David my servant and the Levites who minister before me as countless as the stars of the sky and as measureless as the sand on the seashore' (Jer.33:22).

Similarly science once said that the earth was a flat stationary disc, resting on an immovable platform. Job writing in what is possibly the oldest book in the Bible, speaks of God who spreads out the northern skies over empty space; he suspends the earth over nothing' (Job 26:7).

Dr. Nelson Glueck the Jewish archaeologist said, 'The Bible's incredibly correct historical memory has been validated many times over by archaeological discoveries. No discovery that I have made has ever contradicted a Biblical reference.'

In the Bible are mysteries beyond man's conception or invention and it has stood the test of the ages and of the critics and continues to do so. If it had been written by a man as some claim, it would have to be constantly updated - but there is no need. Man would be able to write a better one now in the light of the knowledge he has gained - but he cannot.

Because the Bible is so reliable when it speaks on subjects which are not the main purpose for it being written, I find it perfectly natural to rely on it when it speaks about who God is. On nearly every page of the Bible God shows that he wants to reveal himself to the reader. 'This is what the Lord says' is a phrase which appears over 3,000 times. This means that it is a living, powerful Word. Wherever it goes in the world, darkness is turned into light.

There is a big difference between the books men make and this book of God: this is a book not made by men; it is a book which makes men. Other books were given for our information, but the Bible was given for our transformation.

The Bible, however, is not only readable and reliable, it is also realistic and this can be seen in various ways: (a) it portrays human nature as it really is, and not as we wish it was; (b) it proclaims God's answer in the person of Jesus Christ who died on the cross for our sins and rose again from the dead; (c) it portrays him as one who can be known experimentally in human hearts because he is alive; (d) when its claims are put to the test they are found to be true.

Make no mistake about it, this is the Word of God. Read it and study it and it will mould your Christian life and enable you to grow as a Christian.

Bible study

Now comes the all-important question as to how you should read the Bible. The simple answer is: regularly and systematically. That is not to suggest that if you have recently become a Christian you should open it at the first chapter of the book of Genesis and read on through until you come to the last chapter of Revelation. When you have become established in your Christian life this can be a good thing.

Start with a New Testament book, for example, the Gospel of Mark, and each day read a chapter, or even part of a chapter. Before reading your section for the day, pray and ask God to help you understand his Word. As you read, keep in mind three questions that you should be constantly asking yourself: (1) What does it say? (2) What does it mean? (3) How does it apply to me?

Sometimes it is helpful to keep a small notebook by you as you read your Bible. Write down any thoughts that come to you as you read. It could be some promise of God to lay hold of. It might be a word of rebuke for you, or some new insight into God's truth. Whatever you read, always seek for some personal application of the Bible to your own heart and life.

When you have tackled several New Testament books then turn to the Old Testament and read your way through one of the books. Possibly you might like to start with the book of Psalms because each Psalm is complete in itself and very much relates to life.

A number of Christian organisations publish Bible Study Notes that can be of help to you in getting to know the Bible and its message. Most of them consist of a portion of the Bible to read and some brief explanatory notes. The best notes are those that follow a systematic plan of reading, usually through a book at a time. To find out what might suit you best, have a look in your local Christian bookshop or better still ask your pastor or church leader for advice.

However helpful Bible Study Notes may be in getting you started in the right direction, the best way to read God's Word is to read a daily section direct from the Bible and then ask God to speak to you through what you have just read. In other words, start digging out your own spiritual treasure. Nobody ever outgrows the Bible. The book widens and deepens with our years. Drink deep at this fountain of knowledge - don't just gargle!

As well as reading the Bible you will also, I hope, want to study the Bible. In this connection it is advisable to use a translation rather than a paraphrase. In addition to the *Authorised Version* there is the *New King James Version* and the *New International Version*. If you are not familiar with the Bible then my personal recommendation would be to use the New International Version.

One of the most useful aids for Bible Study is a concordance. A concordance lists most of the words in the Bible in alphabetical order, so you can look up where the same word is used elsewhere in the Bible. There are also a number of one volume commentaries on the Bible that can be helpful to give you a bird's- eye view of its books. For detailed study, however, it is usually best to purchase commentaries on individual books of the Bible. The local Christian bookshop manager and the pastor of your church will give you good advice about which commentaries might be most helpful to you at this stage in your Christian experience.

Don't be afraid to mark your Bible. Purchase

a set of coloured pencils for this purpose and even scribble notes in the margin if there is room. In addition, do try to memorize verses from the Bible, or even whole chapters, if possible. When John Ruskin was a small boy, his mother insisted on him memorizing seventeen chapters of the Bible and eight Psalms. When he was 55 years old, Ruskin looked back on those days and said that his mother's insistence that he memorize these chapters, 'established my soul for life.'

Sir Wilfred Grenfell, a medical missionary to Labrador said, 'To me, the memorizing of Scripture has been an unfailing help in doubt, anxiety, sorrow, and all the countless vicissitudes of life. I believe it enough to have devoted many hours to stowing away passages of the Scripture in my mind. Facing death on a floating piece of ice on a frozen ocean, I found that recalling the Scriptures supplied solace for my fearful soul.'

Writing out verses of Scripture on small cards and keeping them in your jacket or handbag means that you can slip them out in spare moments and commit them to memory.

Now we must ask, when should you read your Bible? Obviously daily, but as to when in the day, it is really up to you to find the time that suits you best. There is no particular merit in rising early in the morning or in staying up late at night.

What is important is that you set a specific time aside for the reading of God's Word. Your job, home circumstances, your body's needs (some people find that early in the morning they are wide awake, whilst others find that they can concentrate best at night) will determine what time of day you set aside. The only rule for you as a Christian is to find the time that is best for you. Guard this time because the Devil will do his best to keep you from reading God's Word. He knows just how important Bible reading and study are for spiritual growth.

It has often been stressed that the Bible will keep you from sin, but sin will keep you from the Bible. Bishop Wilberforce once said, 'There are four things we ought to do with the Word of God.

(1) Admit it to be the Word of God.
(2) Commit it to our hearts and minds.
(3) Submit to its authority.
(4) Transmit it into our lives.'

There is no question but that regular Bible reading and study go hand in hand with balanced and steady spiritual growth.

COMMUNICATE

3
COMMUNICATE

One of the easiest subjects to write about is prayer, yet to really pray is one of the most difficult things in the world. It is also one of the most essential. 'To be a Christian without praying,' wrote Martin Luther, 'is no more possible than to be alive without breathing.'

But our need to pray is linked to the power it unwinds and makes available to the Christian. John R. Mott said, 'Prayer is the greatest force we can wield' and he went on to add that 'God has given this weapon to every Christian no matter how short a time you have been a Christian.'

God has so planned it that prayer is the chief agency and activity whereby men align themselves with God's purposes. Prayer does not consist of battering the walls of heaven for personal benefits or the success of our own plans. Rather it is the committing of ourselves to God for the carrying out of his purposes. It is a telephone call to Headquarters for orders. It is not a bending of God's will to ours, but our will to God's.

So there are several things that I want to discuss

about prayer as we consider its importance for Christian growth.

Why is prayer important?

Firstly, the person who calls us to pray is the Lord himself. Jesus made this quite clear when he said to his disciples that 'they should always pray and not give up' (Luke 18:1). On many occasions in his letters to some of the young churches of the New Testament, Paul underlines this truth, and he was not just giving his own personal opinion, but rather was writing under divine inspiration. To the Ephesians he says, 'always keep on praying for all the saints' (Eph.6:18); to the Philippians, he writes, 'in everything, by prayer...' (Phil.4:6); to the Thessalonians he says, 'pray continually' (1 Thess. 5:17). These and many other Scriptures indicate that God wants us to be men and women of prayer and to communicate with him often. Remember the words of Philip Brooks: 'Prayer is not conquering God's reluctance, but taking hold of God's willingness.' The one who wants us to 'always pray and not give up' is our Lord Jesus Christ himself.

Secondly, the place of prayer in the life of a Christian should be of first importance for prayer has numerous functions and is God's chosen pathway for giving blessings to his children.

Chiefly it is God's way for Christians to receive from him. James puts this truth very powerfully when he says, 'You do not have, because you do not ask God' (James 4:2). Mark Hopkins said, 'Our prayer and God's mercy are like two buckets in a well; while the one ascends the other descends.' We can pray, believe and receive, or we can pray, doubt and do without. Our God does have boundless resources and the only limit is in us. Our 'requests', our 'thoughts', our 'prayers' are too small. Our expectations are too limited. C.H. Spurgeon likened fervent prayer to the rope in a belfry: 'Prayer pulls the rope below, and the great bell rings above in the ears of God. Some scarcely stir the bell, for they pray so languidly; others give but an occasional pluck at the rope; but he who wins heaven is the man who grasps the rope and boldly pulls continually with all his might.'

Prayer is also God's way to fullness of joy. Jesus said, 'Until now you have not asked for anything in my name. Ask and you will receive, and your joy will be complete'(John 16:24). Philip Melanchthon's testimony bears this out: 'Trouble and perplexity drive me to pray, and prayer drives away perplexity and trouble and ministers joy.'

Prayer is also important in that it is God's way for making Christians free from worry and anxious care. David the Psalmist was fully aware of this and he often testified God answered his prayers when he was in difficulties. 'This poor man called, and the Lord heard him; he saved him out of all his troubles' (Psalm 34:6). This truth is underlined again when David says, 'Cast your cares on the Lord and he will sustain you' (Psalm 55:22). David did not ask for everything to be easy but he knew who had the strength to protect him when his worry and anxiety were very great.

Paul similarly knew the provision of God through prayer. From prison in Rome he wrote to Christians in Philippi: 'Do not be anxious about anything, but in everything, by prayer and petition, with thanksgiving, present your requests to God. And the peace of God, which transcends all understanding, will guard your hearts and your minds in Christ Jesus' (Phil.4:6,7).

Nothing is too much for God to handle. Nothing is too insignificant for him to care about. Henry Beecher explained the universality of these facts when he said, 'Prayer covers the whole of a man's life.' He went on to elaborate: 'There is no thought, feeling, yearning, or desire however low, trifling or vulgar we may deem it, which if it affects our real interest or happiness, we may not lay before God and be sure of sympathy. His nature is such that our coming often does not tire him.

The whole burden of the whole life of every man may be rolled on to God and not weary him, though it has wearied the man.'

Thou art coming to a King,
Large petitions with thee bring,
For his grace and power are such,
None can ever ask too much.

In addition, prayer is of first importance because it is the means by which the Holy Spirit is outpoured. Jesus said, 'Your Father in heaven will give the Holy Spirit to those who ask him' (Luke 11:13). Jesus promised his disciples prior to his ascension: 'But you will receive power when the Holy Spirit comes on you; and you will be my witnesses' (Acts 1:8). After Jesus went back to heaven they returned to Jerusalem and we then read, 'they went upstairs ...where they were staying... and they all joined together constantly in prayer' (Acts 1:13,14). Their prayers were answered and on the Day of Pentecost just a few weeks later they were all filled with the Holy Spirit.

Prerequisites for prayer

There are two basic prerequisites for prayer. Firstly, a holy life. The Psalmist says, 'If I had cherished sin in my heart, the Lord would not have listened... and heard my voice in prayer' (Psalm 66:18,19). You cannot come to God in a bad spiritual condition and expect him to hear and answer your prayers. Thomas Brooks wrote: 'God hears no more than the heart speaks: and if the heart be dumb, God will certainly be deaf.'

Paul lays down clear guidelines for knowing the will of God and therefore praying in that will:

> Therefore, I urge you, brothers, in view of God's mercy, to offer your bodies as living sacrifices, holy and pleasing to God - which is your spiritual worship. Do not conform any longer to the pattern of this world, but be transformed by the renewing of your mind. Then you will be able to test and approve what God's will is - his good, pleasing and perfect will (Rom. 12:1,2).

Here in this Scripture you will discover first of all an obligation: *offer your bodies*. Then follows a condition, *holy and acceptable to God*; and finally, a wonderful outcome: *you will test and approve what God's will is*. A holy life is a necessity for an effective prayer life.

The second prerequisite for prayer to be answered is a pure motive. We constantly need to search our motives when we pray. Am I praying with my own selfish interests in mind? If my

prayer is answered would it make my life easier?
Are you praying for the conversion of your parents, or your husband or wife so that life will be
more comfortable for you? If you are, then your
motivation is wrong. You should be praying for
them because they are lost to God and need to be
found by him.

Practical procedure

In this third section, I want to look at some practical procedures in prayer. Although praying on
your own is the foundation for an effective prayer
life, it is also the hardest form of prayer. Jesus
spoke of its importance when he said: 'When you
pray, go into your room, close the door and pray
to your Father who is unseen. Then your Father,
who sees what is done in secret, will reward you'
(Matt. 6:6). John Berridge wrote out of his own
experience: 'All decay begins in the closet; no
heart thrives without much secret converse with
God - and nothing will make amends for it.'

As with Bible reading, you must set aside a time
each day to pray on your own, and usually it is best
to have this very personal time when you read
God's Word. You can be sure that you will never
find the time, so you must make time. The privacy
of your own room is obviously an ideal location,
but for some young people who share a room with

a brother or sister, this may not be possible. You should be able to find somewhere to be quiet with the Lord. When I was a student at college, in the summer months I would climb up a nearby hill every evening after tea and have my quiet time - so make a time and find a place.

The physical posture is not of prime importance when you pray. You may kneel down with the head lowered, or stand with hands raised to heaven. Most people find that closing the eyes helps concentration, although I must say that some of my most precious times of prayer are when I am driving my car down the motorway late at night - and I certainly do not close my eyes when I am driving! Praying out loud, even though in no more than a whisper also helps to keep your mind from wandering. Other aids to prayer can be a hymn book (many hymns are just prayers set to music) and a prayer book.

I find that a simple note book is helpful for me, with a page for each day of the week on which I list items for prayer. Such a list can include the names of relatives and friends, missionaries, the pastor of your church and others. Such a simple procedure will help you to pray for them regularly. Use the television news reports or the daily papers as prayer reminders. Also, jot down in your notebook things that are happening in the world that call for urgent prayer. It always helps to change the list around after a few months as this helps to keep you fresh in praying. Also, when you do pray privately, don't concentrate just on asking! Do remember to say 'thank you' often.

One helpful exercise is to write down in your prayer notebook on at least one day of the week all of the things that you have to thank God for on that day or week. It can be a very necessary thing to do when you have had many days at prayer just asking God for things without a lot of thanking! In addition, if you find length of time a problem, F.B. Meyer suggests that 'if you can't pray a lot a long time, pray your little a lot.'

As well as praying on your own, the Bible strongly advocates praying with another like-minded person. Jesus promised: 'If two of you on earth agree about anything you ask for, it will be done for you by my Father in heaven' (Matt. 18:19). If there are two of you in one family who are Christians, then pray together. When friends call at your home, pray with them before they leave. Before you say goodnight to your girl or boy friend, pray together. Praying with some other like-minded person can be a real blessing to you and of untold blessing to those you pray for at such times. Seek out someone to pray with, and claim this promise of the Lord Jesus.

Attendance at the meetings for prayer arranged by your own church are obviously very important. As you read through the Book of Acts you will see just what happened when those early Christians prayed together. When the Church was born on the day of Pentecost in Jerusalem, we read that 'they devoted themselves to the apostles teaching and to the fellowship, to the breaking of bread and to prayer' (Acts 2:42). As a Christian you should make it a priority to attend your own church prayer meeting whenever possible.

One of the greatest chapters in the Bible on prayer is Luke 11. As we look at it we notice that the narrative starts with the disciples of Jesus asking their master, 'Lord, teach us to pray.' From this request came the well-known answer of Jesus. This prayer is commonly known as the Lord's Prayer, but it is really the prayer that Jesus taught his disciples to pray and not the prayer that he prayed himself. As you read it you will discover seven great truths about prayer.

The Lord's Prayer (Luke 11:2-4)

The first great truth that this prayer indicates is *our relationship to God*: 'Our Father!' When you come to pray as a Christian you are coming to speak to and to be with your Father, and in this relationship he wants you to enjoy all the privileges of sonship. It is never difficult in a healthy human relationship for a child to talk to his father. How much more should we eagerly want to come into the presence of our heavenly Father and talk to him.

The prayer also speaks to us of *a refuge*. Where is our Father? In heaven. The Bible teaches us that as Christians we have a heavenly refuge, and that refuge is in Jesus Christ. It is as we go to the place of prayer that we begin to enjoy a foretaste of our heavenly refuge. Prayer will lift us above the circumstances and pressures of life and set us free in our spirits.

Some years ago I was leading a House Party in Austria. How thrilling it was to stand in some of those beautiful valleys and gaze up at the towering mountains which disappeared from view into the clouds above. During the holiday, some brave folk attempted to climb some of the mountains. My only attempt was made in a cable car!

However, one lovely crisp January afternoon I was flying back from Athens on a Boeing 737 Jet and flying over part of Austria. How different the mountains looked from five miles high - so small and insignificant because they were now being looked at from a different viewpoint - from above and not from below. This is what prayer can do for you as a Christian. It can lift you up above yourself and the circumstances of your life, and you begin to see things differently as you see them from God's perspective.

Also this prayer speaks to us of *the need for reverence*. As God's people we need to have the right attitude in prayer. It is good to remember that although in prayer you come to God in the intimate relationship of a child to his father, yet you are also coming into the presence of the God and Creator of the universe. 'Father, hallowed be your name' is the right approach.

Now the meaning of the word 'hallowed' is very simply to 'sanctify' or 'to set apart.' This meaning comes out very clearly in the use of the word in Scripture. 'The Lord blessed the Sabbath day and made it holy (he hallowed it)' (Exodus 20:11). He set it apart as distinct and different.

But how do we practically hallow God's name? It is hallowed when our behaviour is such as glorifies him. Peter says, 'But in your hearts set apart Christ as Lord. Always be prepared to give an answer to everyone who asks you to give the reason for the hope that you have. But do this with gentleness and respect' (1Peter 3:15).

Another truth demonstrated to us in the Lord's Prayer is that of a *Rock that is unshakeable*. 'Rock' is one of the Old Testament titles for the Lord - 'The Lord is my rock' (Psalm 18:2). Prayer can certainly be a place of great encouragement as we realise that God is building a Kingdom and the foundation of his Kingdom is Jesus Christ himself: 'Your Kingdom come,' we pray. Jesus made this quite clear, when, in reply to Peter's great affirmation that Jesus was the Christ, he said, 'On this rock I will build my church, and the gates of Hades will not overcome it' (Matt.16:18).

Jesus is not only the foundation stone, he is also the one who is responsible for the formation of the Kingdom. Listen to what he says: 'I will build *my* church' (Matt.16:18). Psalm 127:1 makes it quite clear that 'unless the Lord builds the house, its builders labour in vain.' The future of God's kingdom is assured. Yet if God's Kingdom is to come, then God's will must be done on earth as in heaven, and his will on earth seems to be often related to prayer. As you pray, you will not only begin to see things from God's viewpoint, but you will also begin to realise your own personal responsibility in the work of the Kingdom of God. What an amazing task! What a great God we have that our prayers should have a direct bearing on the final appearance of his Kingdom. The outcome should be that you will do what Jesus said - 'always pray and not give up' (Luke 18:1)

In this prayer we also find a need for *the replenishment of our daily needs*: 'Give us each day our daily bread.' Yes, God is concerned about your daily material needs, so do pray about them. God loves to hear, to answer and provide. He does not promise to supply all that we want, but he does promise to supply all that we need.

If this prayer speaks of provision for material needs, it also names our greatest need, *the remission of sins*: 'Forgive us our sins.' God is willing and able to forgive us as we come to him in repentance and faith. 'If we confess our sins,' says John, 'he is faithful and just and will forgive us our sins and purify us from all unrighteousness' (1 John 1:9). Forgiveness is God's wonderful free gift for all of his believing and trusting people, and what makes it so wonderful is that it is totally unmerited and all of God's grace and mercy.

This prayer also speaks to us of the ability of God to *rescue us in the hour of temptation* when we pray: 'Lead us not into temptation.' There is a wonderful promise in 1 Corinthians 10:13 that God has given to us for our encouragement and help when we face temptation:

No temptation has seized you except what is common to man. And God is faithful; he will not let you be tempted beyond what you can bear. But when you are tempted, he will also provide a way out so that you can stand up under it.'

Let us look again at Luke 11:5-8.

Then (Jesus) said to them, "Suppose one of you has a friend, and he goes to him at midnight and says, 'Friend, lend me three loaves of bread, because a friend of mine on a journey has come to me, and I have nothing to set before him.'

Then the one inside answers, 'Don't bother me. The door is already locked, and my children are with me in bed. I can't get up and give you anything.' I tell you, though he will not get up and give him the bread because he is his friend, yet because of the man's boldness he will get up and give him as much as he needs."

This story contains four features of what prayer is really all about: (1) he revealed a need: he had no bread in the house, and he asked for the need to be met from an outside source; (2) he sought for help because of a relationship: he asked help from a friend; (3) he was specific in his request, 'Lend me three loaves'; (4) he was persistent in his request until help was given.

Jesus, having told the story, now applies it in the context of prayer and exhorts his disciples :

Ask and it will be given to you; seek and you will

find; knock and the door will be opened to you. For everyone who asks receives; he who seeks finds; and to him who knocks, the door will be opened' (Luke 11:9,10).

Effective prayer consists of asking, seeking and knocking.

The human personality similarly, has three avenues of expression - heart, mind and will - and all three play a vital part in real, effective prayer, whether you are praying alone or with others.

There is first of all the prayer of the heart: 'ask and it will be given to you.' Here is the easiest stage of prayer because having a conscious need you come to God in prayer for help. This truth comes out clearly in the story Jesus told: 'Friend, lend me three loaves of bread' (v.5). He had a need, so he asked for help. God certainly wants you to come in prayer to him when you have needs that are beyond your resources to deal with, for his resources are unlimited.

Next comes the prayer of the mind: 'seek and you will find.' This prayer involves the understanding, a searching into the mind and will of God. In Jeremiah 29:12,13, God says, 'Then you will call upon me and come and pray to me, and I will listen to you. You will seek me and find me when you seek me with all your heart.' The man in

Jesus' story, not only came to ask his friend for three loaves, but he gave an explanation (v.6). God wants your prayer life to involve your understanding.

Lastly, there is the involvement of the will in your prayer life: 'knock and the door will be opened to you.' Persistence should characterise prayer as again the story that Jesus told illustrates: 'Because of the man's persistence he will get up and give him as much as he needs' (v.8). God wants you to be persistent in prayer and not to give up. How do our wills function? They operate through a combination of choice and perseverance, and the latter is possibly the harder to put into operation. So choose to pray and keep on praying. If you want to grow as a Christian then you must learn to pray, and the best way to learn is to pray!

One day when Sir Walter Raleigh made a request of her majesty, Queen Elizabeth I, she petulantly said, 'Raleigh, when will you leave off begging?' Sir Walter replied, 'When your majesty leaves off giving.' And our God delights to keep on giving, so keep on asking, seeking and knocking. We should 'always pray and not give up.'

4

TESTINGS, TRIALS AND TEMPTATIONS

If you were not aware of testings, trials and temptations before you became a Christian, I am sure that you are well aware of them now that you have come to Christ and trusted him as your Saviour and Lord. Furthermore, there will be no time in your Christian life and experience when you will be exempt. The temptations of youth give way to those of middle age, and even old age has its own peculiar temptations, because although temptation is something we must never excite, it is something we must always expect.

Henry Law, the nineteenth century preacher, in a fascinating book entitled *The Gospel in Genesis* says of the Devil's ceaseless activity:

He never slumbers, never is weary, never relents, never abandons hope. He deals his blows alike at childhood's weakness, youth's inexperience, manhood's strength and the totterings of old age. He watches to ensnare the morning thought. He departs not with the shade of night. By his legions he is everywhere, at all times. He enters the palace, the fortress, the camp and the fleet. He is busy with the busy. He sits by each bed of sickness, and whispers into each dying ear! Temptation will never leave us until we are ushered into God's presence.

But maybe we ought to start by making it quite clear that there is a difference between trials and temptations, for although God may sometimes test and try us, he never tempts us. In trials he always has as his objective the spiritual development of our character. On the other hand, Satan is the author of temptation and his purpose is that we might fall and experience degradation. God may call you to endure difficulties, but he will never cause you to experience defeat, because the trials of life are meant to make us better Christians and not bitter complainers.

So trials will come. The trials of life can come in various shapes and sizes. Sickness may overtake us, and in today's market economy, so may unemployment or redundancy. Mishap or accident may be our experience and not always of our own making, but as Mae Nicholson said, 'A Christian should never let adversity get him down except on his knees.' God's purposes are always positive, and that is to make us and not break us. Stephen Charnock wrote: 'We often learn more under the rod that strikes us, than under the staff that comforts us!'

Joseph - tested, tried and tempted

One of the great Bible characters who experienced trials and temptation over a long period of time was Joseph. Born into a large family he was at an early age hated by his brothers. One day he was sent by his father to visit his brothers. When they saw him they decided to get rid of him - to murder him! Reuben, however, pleaded for his life and so they put him instead into a pit, only eventually to sell him as a slave to some passing traders who took him down to the slave markets of Egypt.

To be attacked and mistreated by strangers must be traumatic, but to suffer all that he did at the hands of his own brothers must have been horrendous. But as C.H. Spurgeon reminds us, 'Stars may be seen from the bottom of a deep well, when they cannot be discerned from the top of a mountain. So are many things learned in adversity, which the prosperous man dreams not of.' Family betrayal can be a great test of your faith, but looking back on the experience later in life, Joseph stated: 'But God intended it for good' (Gen. 50:20).

Bought in the slave market by a high Egyptian

official, Joseph soon excelled himself and quickly was given great responsibility in his master's household. It was in this position as we shall see later on in another chapter that he faced severe sexual temptation. His master's wife wanted him to go to bed with her, but he refused resolutely. On returning home one night his master was told by his wife that Joseph had tried to rape her. Angrily, he had Joseph thrown into prison on a completely false charge. Can there be anything worse than being accused of immorality when you know that you are totally innocent? Such a horrifying experience must have been a great test of Joseph's faith, but even when looking back on this experience he said, 'But God intended it for good.'

Down in the Egyptian prison God again prospered Joseph: 'the Lord was with him; he granted him favour in the eyes of the prison warder. So the warder put Joseph in charge of all those held in the prison, and he was made responsible for all that was done there' (Gen.39:21,22). During this period the cupbearer and the baker of Pharaoh's court were out of favour with their master and joined Joseph in prison. After they had been in custody some time, and under Joseph's jurisdiction, they both had a dream. One morning Joseph noticed how sad they were and asked them what the problem was. They both told him what they had dreamed. He immediately gave them the meaning of their dreams. The baker was to be hanged and the cupbearer to be reinstated to his former office.

When Joseph informed the cupbearer of his imminent release he added rather feelingly, 'When all goes well with you, remember me and show me kindness; mention me to Pharoah and get me out of this prison. For I was forcibly carried off from the land of the Hebrews, and even here I have done nothing to deserve being put in a dungeon' (Gen.40:14-15). But how sad to read later on that, 'The chief cupbearer, however, did not remember Joseph; he forgot him' (Gen.40:23).

To realise you are forgotten or ignored by somebody who could have been of real help to you can be a real test and trial of your faith. Peter Marshall once said, 'God will never permit any troubles to come upon us unless he has a specific plan by which great blessing can come out of the difficulty.' The Lord does not take us as his servants into deep water to drown us but rather to develop us.

Even after this heartbreaking experience Joseph looked back and said, 'But God intended it for good.' A family betrayal, a false charge of immorality, all were part and parcel of a life being tested and tried, and such trials were actually the structural steel that went into building his character. John Hercus reminds us, 'The great blows of God are designed to make a man stand up.' Joseph certainly responded positively to the blows of trial and God ultimately used him as the human provider for his people Israel. He proved beyond doubt that trials are only to assure us of God's gracious interest in our higher, spiritual welfare. He always has a purpose of grace in all of them.

There is no question but that trials faced and surmounted can be a real benediction. James says, 'Consider it pure joy, my brothers, whenever you face trials of many kinds... Blessed is the man who perseveres under trial' (James 1:2,12).

Temptation - who's behind it all?

From testings and trials I want to move on and look at temptation itself. Sometimes we meet it head on, but on other occasions it is much more subtle. John Bunyan puts it quaintly when he says, 'Temptations when we first meet them are as the lion that roared upon Samson: if we overcome them, the next time we see them we shall find a nest of honey within them.' Temptation succumbed to brings defeat, tragedy and unhappiness, and it is a sad thing when a Christian knows little or nothing of victory over temptation in his life. It was Billy Sunday, the American Evangelist, who said, 'Temptation is the Devil looking through the keyhole, but yielding is opening the door and inviting him in.'

In his remarkable book, *The Christian in Complete Armour,* William Gurnall writes:

If you lean on the window to hear temptation's serenade, Satan is satisfied that his suggestions may at last be taken. If you don't wish to yield to sin, you must be careful not to walk or sit at the door of the occasion. Do not look on temptation with a wandering eye if you do not wish to be taken by it, nor allow your mind to dwell on that which you do not want lodged in your heart.

Satan has no doubt already told you on occasions when you have been tempted and even fallen, that you cannot be a Christian, otherwise you would not be tempted so much. However, take heart for the Bible makes it quite clear that temptation of itself is not sinful. The Bible says of the Lord Jesus, ' We have one who has been tempted in every way, just as we are - yet was without sin' (Heb.4:15). And you can read about the severity of his temptation in Matthew 4:1-11.

Many of God's choicest servants have been greatly tempted. Martin Luther said, 'My temptations have been my masters in divinity.' For nothing is so conducive to real humility as temptation, because it teaches us just how weak we are. The great apostle Paul said of himself on one occasion that he 'served the Lord with great humility and with tears, although I was severely tested by the plots of the Jews' (Acts 20:19). So please do remember that temptation of itself is not sinful.

If you read the account of the temptation of Jesus in Matthew, you will discover just who is behind every temptation. 'Then Jesus was led by the Spirit into the desert to be tempted by the Devil' (Matt.4:1) We must never blame God for our temptation, for as James says, 'When tempted, no one should say, "God is tempting me." For God cannot be tempted by evil, nor does he tempt anyone; but each one is tempted when, by his own evil desire, he is dragged away and enticed' (James 1:13,14). God will sometimes test you, even allow Satan to try you, but God himself will never tempt you.

The tactics of Satan

The methods of temptation which Satan uses have not changed through the centuries, so, being aware of them, it should be possible to prepare for them. So let me share with you four ways in which Satan will bring temptation to you.

Speaking broadly Satan brings temptation to you through what the Bible speaks of as the 'world' - that is, organised society with God left out of its reckoning. John writes of this: 'For everything in the world - the cravings of sinful man, the lust of his eyes and the boasting of what he has and does - comes not from the Father but from the world' (1 John 2:16).

More specifically, Satan sometimes makes a direct attack upon your soul as he did in the case of Jesus. 'The tempter came to him and said, "If you are the Son of God, tell these stones to become bread" ' (Matt.4:3) There is no question but that the Devil will come to you and try to shake your faith and confidence in God's Word and his promises to you. Satan wants to rob you of your assurance. He will seek to mar your conduct as he did in the case of Peter when he succeeded in getting him to deny his Lord at the accusation of a servant girl.

Satan will also use evil spirits and powers which he controls to bring temptation across your path:

For our struggle is not against flesh and blood, but against the rulers, against the authorities, against the powers of this dark world and against the spiritual forces of evil in the heavenly realms (Eph.6:12).

Satan will also use the 'flesh'. Every Christian has two natures. There is, first of all, the natural life that you were born with which is sinful and opposed to God. When you became a Christian, God gave you a new life - his life. Both of these natures are diametrically opposed to one another and clash with each other. Paul describes this battle in Romans 7:21-23:

So I find this law at work: when I want to do good, evil is right there with me. For in my inner being I delight in God's law; but I see another law at work in the members of my body, waging war against the law of my mind and making me a prisoner of the law of sin at work within my members.

Your adversary, the Devil uses the 'flesh' when he comes to encourage you to care for the old nature and to neglect and starve the new spiritual nature and life that God has given you by his Spirit.

James in his very practical epistle says: 'But each one is tempted when, by his own evil desire, he is dragged away and enticed' (James

1:14). Psychiatrist Dr. Smiley Blanton has said, 'Rationalization is the great narcotic that people use to anaesthetise their consciences to justify yielding to temptation.' An embezzler tells himself he is 'just borrowing' the money and will surely put it back. An unfaithful husband assures himself that what his wife does not know will not hurt her. In a thousand daily temptations from padding the expense account to exceeding the speed limit, the rationalized attitude is, 'Everybody is doing it, why shouldn't I?'

But Satan's objective in whatever way he comes at you is always the same. He wants to draw you away and lead you into sin. He may try to take you by surprise, or if this is not possible he will lay siege to your soul. But whatever his strategy may be, as you look to and trust in your Saviour, Jesus Christ, you can experience victory.

Now one of Satan's main methods of temptation is to make you compromise with either the world or the flesh. You must be determined that you are going to be clear cut and without compromise in all compartments of your Christian life, for compromise is always fatal. Compromise ruined Saul when he refused to go all the way in obedience to God's commands and execute the Amalekites. Compromise led to Samson's moral downfall, and it also led King David into adultery and murder.

Unless you are determined to be ruthless in your separation from the things that you know Satan uses in your life, then you will be drawn away.

Carelessness is one of the most effective ways in which Satan brings temptation across your pathway. He will encourage you to be careless in your devotional life. Jesus emphasised how important it was to be watchful when he said, 'Watch and pray so that you will not fall into temptation' (Matt. 26:41).

David knew something of the danger of being careless in his devotional life when he said, 'I have hidden your word in my heart that I might not sin against you' (Psalm 119:11). When talking of warfare, which is often used as an analogy for the spiritual life, Winston Churchill declared that 'we must always be ready to meet at our average moment anything that any possible enemy might hurl against us at his selected moment.'

Satan will most certainly encourage you to be careless in your Christian walk or manner of life and the Bible speaks to us forcibly as Christians that we are 'to live a life worthy of the calling you have received' (Eph.4:1).

There is one thing, however, which is certain before temptation gives way to sin (remember what we said at the beginning of the chapter that temptation of itself is not sinful): Satan must have your co-operation. It takes two to make a temptation successful, and you are one of the two. It is only when the suggestion of the Devil is welcomed, desired, harboured, yielded to, or acted upon that it becomes sinful. So don't co-operate with temptation; do be watchful.

We have encouragement, however, God has provided all that you need in order that you might be able to successfully resist temptation and we have the promise that 'the Lord knows how to rescue godly men from trials' (2 Peter 2:9).

The way of deliverance

Let me now share with you five requirements that you need to enjoy victory and deliverance when you face temptation.

Know yourself, your weaknesses and personal frailties. The Devil comes to us all in different ways. What is a temptation to me, may be no particular problem to you, and the opposite is also true. But be absolutely certain of this. You have no strength of your own to stand against the wiles of the Devil.

Know your weapons provided for you by the Lord Jesus. In Ephesians 6:13-18, the apostle Paul says:

Put on the full armour of God, so that when the

day of evil comes, you may be able to stand your ground, and after you have done everything, to stand. Stand firm then, with the belt of truth buckled round your waist, with the breastplate of righteousness in place, and with your feet fitted with the readiness that comes from the gospel of peace. In addition to all this, take up the shield of faith, with which you can extinguish all the flaming arrows of the evil one. Take the helmet of salvation and the sword of the Spirit, which is the word of God. And pray in the Spirit on all occasions.

Here are weapons that God has provided for you, so take them up and use them in the hour of temptation.

Know your tactics. Firstly, 'resist the Devil and he will flee from you' (James 4:7) is sometimes the right thing to do. 'It is written...' said Jesus when tempted in the wilderness, and the Devil had no answer when confronted with the 'sword of the Spirit,' the Word of God (Matt.4:4). Jesus never argued or debated with Satan. He just showed him the point of the sword, so be sure that you do likewise.

Secondly, 'flee the evil desires of youth' (2 Tim. 2:22) is on other occasions the right tactic in the face of temptation. Don't stop and fight, but turn and run. Tactics are always important in any battle and they are certainly vital in this spiritual battle in which you are engaged as a Christian. F.B. Meyer warned: 'Christ will not keep us safe if we carelessly and wantonly put ourselves into the way of temptation.'

Know your objective. Victory in every temptation, in every department of life should be your ambition. One reason why so often we do not know the victory is that there are some areas of life where we have secret sins, and over these we are not too concerned about victory. We are more worried, however, about yielding to temptations that are open and evident to all. You can be certain of one thing, you will only know victory in your life when you want to experience it in every department of it. Your objective as a Christian wanting to grow spiritually must be total victory and not partial.

Know your Captain. The Lord Jesus is the captain of your salvation. He is the only one who has met every possible type of temptation and conquered them all. It is as you know him, trust him, rely upon him, and give him full control of your life that you will know complete victory in the hour of temptation. Every temptation is actually an opportunity of getting nearer to God.

I remember a number of years ago hearing a

preacher recount how he faced and found victory when temptation came to him. 'Yes, I do know what it is to be tempted by most of the things that the Devil can bring in front of me,' he said, 'but when temptation knocks at the door of my heart, I simply say to the tempter, "Satan, the place is occupied." ' We need to follow his example, for the Bible says, 'The one who is in you is greater than the one who is in the world' (1 John 4:4).

Socrates once said, 'An unexamined life is not worth living,' and how right he was. It is always true to say that the life worth living is sure to be tested in some way or other. Victories won in the hour of trial and temptation not only strengthen you to face the next ones, but also can be a source of encouragement and strength to other Christians.

Testings, trials and temptations of one kind or another will be your experience through all the days of your Christian life. Face them, surmount them and learn from them in the strength that God can and does supply and then you will find yourself growing as a Christian.

5
FOLLOW THE LEADER

Is God really interested in my life? Has he a plan and a purpose for me? How can I discover God's will for my life? Will God guide me? These are certainly some of the questions that you will be asking from time to time in your Christian life. 'I felt led,' is a phrase we often use. What do we mean? Is it just an empty, meaningless phrase that Christians get into the habit of using, or can we really be led by God in our lives?

A.J. Cronin said, 'Life is no straight and easy corridor along which we travel free and unhampered, but a maze of passages, through which we must seek our way - now lost and confused, now checked in a blind alley. But always God will open a door for us, not perhaps one that we ourselves would ever have thought of, but one that will ultimately prove good for us.' Is he right or wrong? Does God always open a door for us?

There are, of course, many wonderful illustrations in the Bible to encourage us to believe that God does lead and guide. Abraham was told by God: '"Leave your country, your people and your father's household and go to the land I will show you. I will make you into a great nation and I will bless you; I will make your name great and you will be a blessing ..." so Abram left, as the Lord had told him' (Genesis 12:1-4). History testifies to the fact that Abraham's response to God's guidance has brought untold spiritual blessing to countless numbers.

Moses was keeping sheep out on the edge of the desert when God revealed to him what his future ministry was to be: 'I am sending you to Pharaoh to bring my people the Israelites out of Egypt' (Exodus 3:10). Although he initially did not want to respond to God's guidance, when he did obey he discovered just how accurate God's statement was.

You cannot read very far in the Old Testament without coming across the phrase, 'This is what the Lord says', or 'The word of the Lord came unto me saying'. The prophets did not give their own opinions or ideas, or the majority verdict at the end of a committee meeting. They always told the people what God had to say on the matter. By what they said, guidance was given by God to kings, nations, and also to individual men and women.

God speaking in the Psalms says, 'I will instruct you and teach you in the way you should go:

I will counsel you and watch over you' (32:8). Solomon gives to us one of the most beautiful promises in the Bible concerning God's desire to guide and lead us: 'Trust in the Lord with all your heart and lean not on your own understanding; in all your ways acknowledge him, and he will make your paths straight' (Proverbs 3:5,6). God's promise to his people is, 'Whether you turn to the right or to the left, your ears will hear a voice behind you, saying, "This is the way; walk in it" ' (Isaiah 30:21).

Once you come into the New Testament you will speedily discover that our God is interested and concerned about the most minute details of your life. Matthew reminds us that 'God clothes the grass of the field' (6:30) and 'even the very hairs of your head are all numbered' (10:30). Jesus said, 'Are not two sparrows sold for a penny? Yet not one of them will fall to the ground apart from the will of your Father' (Matt.10:29).

Now if God shows interest in these apparently insignificant details of life and human experience, how much more interested must he be in the path which our lives take.

Writing to the Colossian Christians, Paul said, 'Since the day we heard about you, we have not stopped praying for you and asking God to fill you with the knowledge of his will through all spiritual wisdom and understanding' (1:9). In Ephesians we are reminded that not only does God reveal his will to us, but also commands us to understand it (5:17). But although God wants us to know his will for us, and will reveal it to us, he will not force it upon us. If we do not diligently seek and listen carefully, we will miss it.

Nothing is right for a Christian if it is not God's will for him. So as we consider how we can individually know God's guidance in our lives, may we look at it under two headings. Firstly, some general principles of guidance, and secondly, on a more personal note.

Some general principles of guidance
God guides us by his Word, the Bible. For God to do that, we will need to read it regularly and systematically. Paul reminded Timothy:

All Scripture is God-breathed and is useful for teaching, rebuking, correcting and training in righteousness, so that the man of God may be thoroughly equipped for every good work' (2 Tim. 3:16,17).

As we dig into God's Word, we discover that most of God's will for our lives in its basic foundation and direction is very clear and direct.

Similarly, in the Old Testament God, by his servant Moses, said to the children of Israel:

Now what I am commanding you today is not too difficult for you or beyond your reach. It is not up in heaven, so that you have to ask, "Who will ascend into heaven to get it and proclaim it to us so that we may obey it?" Nor is it beyond the sea, so that you have to ask, "Who will cross the sea to get it and proclaim it to us so that we may obey it?" No, the word is very near you... so that you may obey it' (Deut. 30:11-14).

Be determined that as a Christian you are going to immerse yourself in God's Word and you will find that God will speak to you and direct you. There will be some thought, phrase or verse that will just stick in your heart and mind and really come alive. It may be that you were converted when some verse from the Bible really reached down deep into your heart, and the same can happen now that you are a Christian. God will use his Word to speak to you, and to show you what you should be.

Then there is of course the Holy Spirit's witness, and that can only be described as an inner voice within which says in effect, 'This is the way.'

Hannah Pearsall Smith in her book, *The Christian's Secret of a Happy Life*, says:

> God's promise is that he will work in us to will as well as to do of his good pleasure. This means, of course that he will take possession of our will, and work it for us; and that his suggestions will come to us, not so much as commands from the outside as desires springing up from within. They will originate in our will: we shall feel as though we desired to do so, not as though we must. We are drawn to obey instead of being driven to it. The way in which the Holy Spirit therefore usually works in a fully obedient soul, in reference to this direct guidance, is to impress upon the mind a wish or desire to do or to leave undone certain things.

God may also guide you through the circumstances in which you find yourself at present. Your educational background, job experience, gifts of personality as well as spiritual gifts are usually all factors in God's guidance in your life. If you are tone deaf, it is most unlikely that God will call you to be a gospel singer! Paul said, 'But each man has his own gift from God; one has this gift, another has that' (1 Cor.7:7). It is not a bad thing to evaluate what abilities God has given you. Do you feel called to a public ministry? Then ask your pastor if you can start to teach in the Sunday School. Can you talk to people personally? Then put it into practice. Why not try some door to door visitation?

But having said that this is often God's way, sometimes as in the case of Moses who told God that he was slow of speech and not at all articulate, God will take us in a certain direction and use us despite our natural inabilites.

Some personal requirements for guidance
The first and most obvious requirement is to be absolutely certain that you are in God's family. Are you a child of God, and therefore a Christian? You cannot expect God to guide you if you don't know him. Just as a good human father will give guidance to his own children, we can be certain that our heavenly Father will guide and lead us as his children. God always provides light through every one of his tunnels.

Having established our spiritual parenthood, obedience to God's plainly revealed will in the Bible is absolutely essential if you want God to reveal to you his more specific and personal will for your life. God will not lead you further if you are disobeying a present plain command to you.

'The will of God is not just to understand, it is something we are to undertake' (George Duncan).

Sometimes when there appears to be confusion and frustration concerning the will of God for your life, it is because of disobedience to some plain and obvious commandment of God. God's guidance for our lives will always stop when known sin is present. If God has already made known his will about a certain matter e.g. 'Do not be yoked together with unbelievers'(2 Cor.6:14), and you are courting an unconverted boy or girl friend, then you do not need to pray about or ask anybody else for advice. All you need to do is to be obedient to God and break the relationship.

We must choose this course of obedience or if we are not careful we might find ourselves trying to alter God's will for our lives rather than wanting to discover and obey it. A.W. Tozer said that, 'To will the will of God is to do more than give unprotesting consent to it; it is rather to choose God's will with positive determination.'

Samuel, the Old Testament prophet, started his life of obedience to God when, as a small boy in the household of Eli the priest, God spoke to him during the night. Samuel replied, 'Speak, for your servant is listening.' Sad to say, we often change the order and say to the Lord, 'Listen, Lord, for your servant is speaking.' It was Henry

Drummond who said, 'The end of life is not to do good, although many of us think so. It is not to win souls, although I once thought so. The end of life is to do the will of God whatever it may be.'

So with all of this in mind, it is very important that as you read the Bible day by day, you ask yourself the question, 'Is there anything in what I have read that calls for my obedience?' David testified that God's Word was a 'lamp to his feet and a light for his path' (Psalm 119:105) and although spoken over 3,000 years ago, these words are still a wonderful testimony to the value of the Bible for Divine guidance. You will add your testimony as you follow in the Psalmist's footsteps.

It is my sincere belief that above everything else, God guides us by his Holy Spirit. Day by day you must be careful to 'walk in the Spirit,' and this means obedience to God's Word. God usually of course guides in accordance with his values and not ours, so you must be watchful that you do not 'grieve the Holy Spirit' (Eph. 4:30) by allowing sin dominance in your life. You must seek continually to be 'filled with the Spirit' (Eph. 5:18).

A wholehearted surrender to God is another personal requirement for discovering God's will. Donald Grey Barnhouse claimed from experience that '95% of knowing the will of God consists in being prepared to do it before you know what it is.' Paul certainly underlines this principle:

> Therefore, I urge you, brothers, in view of God's mercy, to offer your bodies as living sacrifices, holy and pleasing to God - that is your spiritual act of worship. Do not conform any longer to the pattern of this world, but be transformed by the renewing of your mind. Then you will be able to test and approve what God's will is - his good, pleasing and perfect will (Rom.12:1,2).

Notice apart from anything else in this verse that discovering and knowing God's will comes *after* we offer ourselves in service and worship to God. When we have heavenly priorities and not earthly ones, then God's purposes will be clear and plain to us.

Paul Rees enunciates the Christian's position: 'To understand the will of God is my problem; to undertake the will of God is my privilege; to undercut the will of God is my peril.' A genuine devotion and wholehearted surrender to God will result in you fulfilling his will at the time, in the situation, and under the circumstances in which *he* has placed you. God's guidance has often got the long term in view and you may have to make a sacrifice now for a gain in the future. One of the greatest benefits of knowing God's guidance is not in what it gives to us or even sends us but rather what it does with us now. As James Jauncy says in *Guidance By God*, 'God's will for tomorrow builds upon God's will fulfilled in our lives today.' Location or future events are not unimportant obviously, but these are not primarily what guidance is all about. Jesus said, 'The work of God is this: to believe in the one *he* has sent' (John 6:29) and this must be our priority. This is the first task we are called to and one which we must continually fulfil.

There is also no doubt that if you are to know God's will for your life, then you must be single-minded in following Christ. The Bible says that a 'double minded man is unstable in all his ways' (James 1:8 A.V.) and Paul underlined this truth when he wrote: 'But one thing I do; forgetting what is behind and straining towards what is ahead, I press on towards the goal' (Phil. 3:13,14). If we deviate from God's will because we are not single-minded then it will certainly mean that we will not only know his second best for our lives, but it could also mean spiritual disaster.

The guidance of God often comes in answer to prayer and supplication, so do pray much about what God wants to do in and with your life. The

Bible promises, 'If any of you lacks wisdom, he should ask God, who gives generously to all without finding fault, and it will be given to him' (James 1:5). Nothing lies beyond the reach of prayer except that which lies outside the will of God.

Following the general principles previously mentioned concerning God's guidance through our abilities and circumstances, it is important to concentrate on what we are given to do and be at present. Often in Scripture we find men and women guided into service while faithfully engaged in the ordinary, every day responsibilities of life. Think of Moses who was out in the wilds of the desert, looking after sheep when God appeared to him at the burning bush and called him to be his mouthpiece to mighty Pharoah.

Be determined that you are going to do well what God has called you to be engaged in now. If you get over-anxious about the future it can so easily paralyse your present responsibilities. God always expects us to carry out our present task with great diligence before he will entrust to us something far greater.

Seeking the godly counsel and help of others can also be most helpful as we wait upon God for his guidance and direction. It can be so encouraging, when you feel God's tug in a certain direction and you share it with the church leadership to find that you have their encouragement and support. Others can pray for you and with you and provide you in some cases with further information and insight. Many of us have discovered that God's guidance is often a progressive thing and not always an instant revelation.

And this leads me to the last personal requirement for guidance: take time and test the guidance of God. John Wesley wrote in his Journal during November, 1759: 'Do not hastily ascribe things to God. Do not suppose dreams, visions, impressions, visions and revelations to all be from God. They may be from him, they may be from nature, they may be from the Devil. Therefore, believe not every spirit, but try the spirits whether they be from God.'

Follow Jesus

One of the surest ways of knowing God's guidance in your life and growing spiritually is to simply 'follow Jesus.' One of the great commands of the Lord Jesus to those who believe in him is precisely this - 'Follow me' (Matt.4:19). In fact as you read through the Gospels you will discover that the word 'follow' with its synonyms is found seventy-seven times. Sifting through all of these references you will discover that there are three basic ways in which we as Christians are called to follow the Lord Jesus in order that we may know God's plan for our lives.

Firstly, we are called to follow Jesus *immediately*. There is a sense of urgency in the call of Jesus, and equally there should be an immediate response. Jesus said, 'Come follow me, and I will make you fishers of men' (Mark 1:17,18).

Secondly, we are called to follow Jesus *closely*. This comes out very clearly in the words of Jesus, 'I have set you an example' (John 13:15). The word 'example' means a 'pattern' or a 'copy'. It was the word used when a teacher drew characters on a scroll, which the pupils had to copy, and get as close to as possible.

God's pattern for the Christian is the Lord Jesus Christ, and you are to follow him and seek to be like him. The Bible says, 'Let us run with perseverance the race marked out for us. Let us fix our eyes on Jesus' (Heb.12:1,2). This is again underlined by Peter: 'Christ suffered for you, leaving you an example that you should follow in his steps' (1 Peter 2:21).

Thirdly, we are to follow Jesus *fully*. If the call of Christ is anything at all it is a call to a whole-hearted commitment with no reserves, holding nothing back. 'If anyone would come after me, he must deny himself and take up his cross daily and follow me' (Luke 9:23). And make no mistake about it, to follow Jesus fully can be exceedingly costly.

On one occasion Jesus was answering the question of a man who wanted to know what he had to do to inherit eternal life. 'Jesus looked at him and loved him. "One thing you lack," he said. "Go, sell everything you have and give to the poor, and you will have treasure in heaven. Then come, follow me." At this the man's face fell. He went away sad, because he had great wealth' (Mark 10:21-22). The man could not face the cost.

Said General Sharp of the U.S. Marine Corps, 'If in this troubled world we can produce enough God-guided men and women, then we would not need guided missiles!' Heaven is waiting to help those who will discover God's will and then do it. Follow the Lord Jesus Christ, and you will grow as a Christian.

6
LOVE NOT THE WORLD

We sometimes sing a song, 'This world is not my home, I'm just a passing through,' and as true as that is from one point of view, it is also true to say that at present we are in the world. But one important question that I want us to consider in this chapter is, 'What should our attitude be as Christians to the world in which we live?' How are we to relate to its aims, ambitions, haunts, habits, outlooks, pastimes, pleasures and music? Does it matter what we do, where we go and what we see? Has God given us any help in sorting out these things? The answer is yes - in the pages of the Bible. Answers that are not always specific in detail, but certainly very clear in principle.

Now there are many references in the Bible to the social responsibilities of Christians in the world in terms of relationships with people, society, employers and the Government. As Christians we do have responsibilities in these areas, and throughout history, Christians have been at the forefront in social concern and care, dealing with some aspects of these.

But there is one Biblical word that I want to highlight as we think of the Christian and the world and it is the word *separation:* 'Therefore, come out from them and be separate' (2 Cor.6:17). God calls us as Christians to be a separate people, but what does this mean? How does it apply to us living in today's world with all of its particular problems and perils?

Separation

In the Bible the word 'separate' is used in at least five different ways. It is used first of all of the separation of the sinner from God: 'But your iniquities have separated you from your God' (Isaiah 59:2). It is also used of the separation of Christ from sinners: 'Such a high priest, meets our needs - one who is holy, blameless, pure, set apart from sinners' (Heb.7:26). Again we find it speaking of the separation of Jesus Christ from God when he died on the cross for our sin: 'My God, my God, why have you forsaken me' (Matt. 27:46). And on another occasion it describes the separation of the saved from the lost: 'And besides all this, between us and you a great chasm has been fixed' (Luke 16:26). Last of all, it speaks of the separation of the Christian from the world:

Do not be yoked together with unbelievers. For what do righteousness and wickedness have in common? Or what fellowship can light have with darkness? What harmony is there between Christ and Belial? What does a believer have in common with an unbeliever? What agreement is there between the temple of God and idols? For we are the temple of the living God ... therefore come out from them and be separate, says the Lord' (2 Cor.6:14-17).

Or in other words: be different. The emphasis in all of the New Testament letters is that Christians are to be different from non-Christians, and this, is not only in terms of the inside because we have been born again, but also on the outside affecting how we live in the world. So often we can make the excuse that 'God looks on the heart,' which is true, but it is also true to say that the only difference that the world can see is what is obvious on the outside. Sadly they don't often see very much difference. The Bible's emphasis to us is: be not conformed to this world; be separate. What the New Testament writers are saying to us is that because as Christians we are different from non-Christians, then it should show in a positive way in our lives.

It is certainly not separation in terms of a lack of contact with the world, but rather separation in terms of non-conformity or complicity with the world and its standards, its habits and ambitions which are contrary to God's will and Word. The Lord Jesus Christ put this truth in a nutshell when he pled with his Father:

'My prayer is not that you take them out of the world, but that you protect them from the evil one' (John 17:15).

The world and worldliness

So what is this 'world' that we are to be separate from and different to? Two Greek words are used in the New Testament that have been translated as the one word 'world'. The first one is *aion* and it is the word used to describe a time marked by certain moral characteristics. It is the world where man is exalted and darkness and depravity rule. It is the world where materialism is prized above all else. This is the world which is antagonistic to God. It is the word that Paul uses when he says, 'Do not conform any longer to the pattern of this world, but be transformed by the renewing of your mind' (Romans 12:2).

We are not to be squeezed into the world's shape. We are not to accommodate its standards of morality. Finding out what most people do and then calling it normal is not to be a characteristic of our lives. We must be careful what books and magazines we read, what music we listen to, what films we watch in the cinema or on the TV. Is the subject matter wholesome or does it make a mockery of sin and belittle God's standard? Sin should never be the subject matter of entertainment.

Yes, we all need relaxation and the arts can be a real blessing, but if they portray what is depraved and unclean then they will stunt my spiritual growth as a Christian and I need to separate myself from them. It has been said that a frog placed in tepid water will not move if warmer water is gradually added, until finally it dies from the heat. Similarly, you as a Christian can become so accustomed to evil around you, that but for the grace of God, you would succumb. One way out is not to put yourself on the pathway of difficulty to start with - separate yourself from the world.

The second word used for *world* in the New Testament is *kosmos* and this word has to do with the system and the way that the world is arranged, with greed, selfishness, ambition and covetousness predominating. When writing to the Corinthians, Paul compared this world to the Creator's greatness, 'For the wisdom of the *kosmos* is foolishness in God's sight' (1 Cor. 3:19) and he added that 'this *kosmos* in its present form is passing away' (1 Cor. 7:31), stressing its destructive system and values. To the Christians in Galatia he stressed the sinner's imprisonment in this world: 'so also, when we were children, we were in slavery under the basic principles of the *kosmos* (Gal. 4:3).

Paul is at pains to remind us that we were bound up in this world system, we shared its hopes, enjoyed its pleasures, accepted its standards. But because we have been saved from such a system, we are now to live as those who no longer belong to it - and how is that to be? Separated and different. Lack of separation or worldliness will definitely hinder us in our Christian lives and stunt our spiritual growth.

'Don't you know,' asks James, 'that friendship with the world is hatred towards God. Anyone who chooses to be a friend of the world, (accepts its standards, and adopts its norms of behaviour, or follows its aims), becomes an enemy of God' (James 4:4). The world is the eternal foe of Jesus, and if you are a Christian then it will be your foe as well. The world's constant pull will only undermine your loyalty to Christ.

Worldliness means being overtaken by self indulgence, because behind all worldliness is some expression of the flesh. Our adversary the Devil has a powerful magnet called the 'world' and when he points it at us we can be dragged away from God and service for him, from prayer and from Bible reading. Whatever dulls your spiritual appetite needs to be avoided like the plague. Surrendering to self-indulgence will definitely hinder your spiritual growth.

After being drawn away by self-indulgence you can so easily become enmeshed in earthly things, living as you do in a very materialistic society. Jesus said, 'Watch out! Be on your guard against all kinds of greed; a man's life does not consist in the abundance of his possessions' (Luke 12:15). As Christians you are not to be bound by the temporalities of life. Instead you are to be mastered by the realities of eternity. Paul reminds us, in his letter to the Corinthian believers, that 'this world in its present form is passing away' (1 Cor.7:31). Yet, as true as you know this to be in theory you can easily find yourself caught up with the spirit of covetousness and become discontented with what you have.

In your desire to maintain or improve your standard of living you can so easily make the luxuries of yesterday become the necessities of today. A lot of trouble is caused when your yearnings get ahead of your earnings! A cynic once said, 'Let us all be happy and live within our means, even if we have to borrow money to do it.' But this should never be the approach of a Christian wanting to please God.

It was Epicurus, the Greek Philosopher, who said, 'If you want to make a man happy, add not to his possessions, but take away from him his desires.' In our worldly 'consumer goods-are-all-important' society, we desperately need to cultivate the attitude of the dear old Christian lady who on being taken to a brand new shopping precinct and asked what she thought of it said, 'I don't know when I've seen so many things that I could well do without.' Be very careful that you don't let the accumulation of things cut the nerve of your spiritual life. Worldliness in this area will certainly hinder your Christian growth.

Worldliness will also hinder you as far as serving Christ is concerned. Paul reminded Timothy, 'No one serving as a soldier gets involved in civilian affairs, he wants to please his commanding officer' (2 Tim.2:4). What a tragedy it is that so often Christians think that they have to be like the world in its outlook, habits and lifestyle in order to get a hearing for the gospel. Worldliness would suggest that to be effective you need to walk as close to the edge as possible in order to communicate, whereas the New Testament indicates that you have to keep as far away from the edge as possible. If there is any doubt about anything that you allow in your life, any practice, any experience or pursuit, then always give God the benefit of the doubt and you will never be the loser. When God urges us to be done with worldliness in all of its subtle and not so subtle forms, it is for very good and positive reasons, so let me share one of them with you.

Paul writing to the Philippian Christians reminded them that 'our citizenship is in heaven. And we eagerly await a Saviour from there' (Phil.3:20). All that God has for us of eternal value is in heaven. What we may or may not have on earth does not really matter in the long run, because it has no lasting value anyway. The Bible reminds us that 'what is seen is temporary, but what is unseen is eternal' (2 Cor.4:18).

Our citizenship is in heaven and not upon earth even though of course we have earthly responsibilities as long as we live in the dimension of time. Peter wrote to Christians under real pressure from the society in which they lived said:

Praise be to the God and Father of our Lord Jesus Christ! In his great mercy he has given us ... an inheritance that can never perish spoil or fade - kept in heaven for you (1Peter1:3,4).

In the light of this heavenly citizenship that we have, let us be separate from the world. If you want to grow as a Christian then you must be very careful not to get immersed in worldliness.

7
LOVE, SEX AND MARRIAGE

If there was life on other planets and they sent a visitor to earth, he would certainly come to the conclusion that the time on planet earth was sex-o'clock! Our society seems to be totally obsessed with sex in one form or another. Modern advertising, television commercials, popular music, the cinema, theatre and the printed page offer sex as a bonus with everything from toothpaste to Bounty bars.

Albert Camus the French Philosopher commented:

> Every century of mankind's history seems to be characterized by one specific emphasis. The seventeenth century by Mathematics, the eighteenth century by the Physical sciences, the nineteenth century by Biology.

I think that we could add that the twentieth century is characterized by sex.

We seem to have bred a race of journalists who have consecrated their lives to publicising men and women who have the faces of angels but the morals of alley cats and that might be an insult to cats! In addition, we have a new race of novelists who dredge up literary sludge from the sewers of their minds to provide entertainment for the masses. Best-selling novels have page after page of torrid descriptions of sexual ecstasy.

C.S. Lewis made a very shrewd observation on the sexual titillation of much modern literature, cinema and theatre:

> It is perfectly normal to enjoy food, but there might be good reason to wonder about the person who would stand around with drooling mouth, while someone slowly and slyly drew aside a napkin covering a plate of pork chops, as if by this clandestine, unnatural process, the food was to be enjoyed the more. Yet, this is the attitude towards sex that is so often adopted by much modern literature, cinema, theatre and popular music.

Who invented sex?

So who invented sex? Contrary to popular opinion it was not the brainchild of Hollywood. Make no mistake about it, sex is God's invention, creation and gift, and because everything God does is good, then sex within the right and proper parameters is also good. It was God who implanted physical attraction between the sexes, and if the opposite sex, or at least some of them do not attract you, then take care, for you may have problems.

Sex is not sinful, but rather it is part of God's plan, and as such it is to be accepted with thanksgiving as one of God's most precious gifts. But as we examine it here we shall see that it is not a free for all, suggesting a licence to grab what you can while it is around. As one of God's gifts, sex is to be expressed in accordance with his design for it. In other words, we do have to follow the Maker's instructions, and his instructions in this case are to be found in the Bible.

Now while the Bible does not spell out a detailed theory of sex, it does make various specific references to sex as well as more generally opening up for us a perspective on life as a whole, including our sexuality. In this connection, the Bible is clear in explaining that our bodies must be seen as part of the glorious creation which God called into being and which he redeemed in Jesus Christ.

What is God's plan and purpose for sex?
At the centre of God's guidance on sex stands the directive which has been most frequently broken in past and present societies. This guidance is

simple. It is that sex is ordained by God to occur only within the context of marriage. Premarital sex is a no-go area. Christianity does not say 'No' to sex, it says 'Yes' on the basis of divine creation. But it does say 'No' to premarital sex on the basis of divine authority. It is here of course that Christianity differs from the philosophy which regards sex only as a natural impulse related to nothing ultimately but pleasure and self- gratification.

For although sex is a physical unity, it signifies something far deeper. The divine commentary in Genesis says, 'For this reason a man will leave his father and mother and be united to his wife, and they will become one flesh' (Gen.2:24). The meeting of two bodies of itself is not an expression of love, because love must exist between two persons before sex can fulfil all that God planned it to achieve. Loveless sex only regards a person as a sexual object and such an attitude is unbiblical to say the least, and it destroys respect for the other person. The mystery of our sexuality is one of the deep mysteries of our personhood. The mystery in our own individual selves is compounded by the fact that we are never individuals alone, but are persons only in a relationship.

What about God's purpose for sex? Firstly, it is the means that God has given for the propagation of the human race. When God created Adam and Eve in the beginning, he said to them, 'Be fruitful and increase in number: fill the earth and subdue it. Rule over the fish of the sea and the birds of the air and over every living creature that moves on the ground' (Gen 1:28). Therefore, it gives to a man and a woman an unspeakable privilege, that of sharing with God in the making of a new life. Sex leads to parenthood with all of its responsibilities, and it gives a visible continuity to love.

In addition sex relates to companionship, for it is not a cold, mechanical procedure. Eve was not created for the propagation of the human race alone, because God said, 'It is not good for the man to be alone. I will make a helper suitable for him' (Gen.2:18). But make no mistake about it, sex is also for enjoyment. Nowhere does the Bible restrict sex for the sole purpose of procreation. 'Enjoy life with your wife, whom you love' (Ecc. 9:9). Our sexuality offers us fantastic pleasure. It is God's gift of creative grace that he made our bodies so that they could have and give pleasure.

So here is God's plan and purpose as outlined in the Bible, and we do well to follow the Maker's instructions for our own benefit and blessing.

Jesus' standard on sexual sin

But what does the Bible say to us about sex that is not within Biblical boundaries? Two words are used in the Bible to describe heterosexual sin, (that is sex outside the context of marriage,) and they are the words 'adultery' and 'fornication.' Adultery is the sexual relationship with the wife or husband of another person. Fornication describes the illicit relationship in general between unmarried people - and both are forbidden. In fact, Jesus took the commandment forbidding adultery even further when he said, 'You have heard that it was said, "Do not commit adultery." But I tell you that anyone who looks at a woman lustfully has already committed adultery with her in his heart' (Matt.5:27,28).

When Jesus said, 'If your right eye offends you, pluck it out,' what did he mean? He meant that we should remove from our lives anything that causes us to sin. Deliberate exposure to filth easily leads to mental adultery. There is an old proverb that says, 'He who would not enter the room of sin must not sit at the door of temptation.' You cannot always stop an evil thought from flitting into your mind, but you do not have to keep it, dwell upon it, and chew it over.

The eye-catching sight of an attractive girl is not wrong, for it is perfectly natural to admire beauty. But if you discover the impulse to lust through looking and do not turn away, but cherish a sinful desire, then this is mental adultery and as such it is sin. Strong words, but that is what Jesus said. And ladies, if you dress in such a way that stimulates a fellow to lust after you, then you are equally guilty.

But today's obsession with sex does present a real problem for the person who does want to be pure. For if lustful looks were condemned by Jesus, what sort of judgment would he pronounce upon our society with its sick obsession with sex. How right the Bible has proved to be when, back in Genesis, God said about man 'that every inclination of the thoughts of his heart was only evil all the time' (Gen.6:5).

How can we know victory in this area? What is the answer? For if we are beaten in the area of sex, then we are beaten indeed.

Overcoming sexual temptation

There is a fascinating story in the Bible that I want to explore, because I believe that more than anywhere else in the Scriptures it gives us some help in the whole area of sexual temptation. It is the story of Joseph in Genesis 39. As we discovered in a previous chapter, Joseph finally finishes up in Egypt in the household of a high Egyptian official, having been sold as a slave by his own brothers. God was with Joseph and favoured him and he eventually found himself promoted to be in charge of the whole household. It was in this privileged position that his master's wife sought to seduce him and miserably failed. So what are the important lessons to learn from the experience of Joseph?

First of all, we do need to notice that this sexual temptation came to him at a time in his life when he was very susceptible and most vulnerable to this type of attack. He was a young man between twenty and twenty-five, when sexual temptation is possibly at its strongest and is hardest to resist. There is no doubt from how the Bible describes him (Genesis 39:6 tells us that Joseph was well-built and handsome) that he was physically attractive. He was also a long way from home with no contact with his family and living in an apparently hopeless situation, so who would know if he did succumb? If he gave in to her advances it would certainly put him in good standing with her. And yet, faced with such a temptation and in such a situation, he was able to resist.

To bamboozle Joseph further, this temptation was totally unexpected. As he was busy in the active routine of his daily job he never dreamt that he would come face to face with one of the greatest temptations of his life, but he did, and we need to be aware that sexual temptation is not always predictable. We need to watch our relationships with members of the opposite sex whom we work with day by day. Joseph might have been aware of the temptation which female slaves in the household might present to him, but he certainly could not have thought that his master's wife would confront him in this way.

There was also the added temptation of an easy opportunity: 'One day he went into the house to attend to his duties, and none of the household servants was inside. She caught him by his cloak and said, "Come to bed with me" '(Gen.39:11). She never gave up in trying to get him, but he never gave in, and he was able to resist her continual temptation. He did so, because he took a strong stand against it from the beginning! 'Though she spoke to Joseph day after day, he refused to go to bed with her or even to be with her' (Gen 39:10).

His courteous but firm reply to her is a model for all of us when faced with any sexual temptation. Similarly, his awareness of God's perspective on the matter acts as an example: 'How then could I do such a wicked thing and sin against God' (Gen. 39:9). All sin is against God and it is important to realise this. Sexual sin is also a sin against someone else, as it is a sin against yourself, but first of all, it is a sin against God.

Notice finally what Joseph had to do eventually when confronted with her continual temptation - 'he ran out of the house.' There is a time to stand and resist, but there also comes a time when it is right to turn and run. And running in such a situation is not failure, it is just downright common sense. Paul gave the same good advice to Timothy when he said, 'Flee the evil desires of youth' (2 Tim. 2:22).

As well as this Biblical precept of Paul's there are also some practical things that you can do or not do in order to cope with and overcome sexual temptation. Let me share some of them with you briefly.

Avoid spending too much time alone with your boy or girl friend in a private or secluded place. Make sure that you meet with other groups of young people. If you are always alone together, do not be surprised if you cannot cope with temptation - and do not go upstairs to the bedroom to talk or listen to records.

Be slow and careful about physical contact. One of the sad things noticeable today is how quickly many young people establish physical contact even though they have hardly been introduced to each other. It is sometimes embarrassing to watch some young couples in public as they appear to be rambling over each other with an ordnance survey map!

God has of course made us so that we attract and are attracted. He has given us powers within that if wrongly stirred can be dynamite, but if rightly harnessed can be sheer delight. Sex can be a wonderful servant, but it can be a terrible master. Be determined that it will be your servant and then it will occupy its rightful, God-given place in your life and not hinder your growth as a Christian.

Marriage and family life

Marriage and family life is God's normal plan for most of us, but if this is not to be his plan for you, then you can be sure that he has something better and more fulfilling as far as you are concerned.

One thing I do want to outline in connection with marriage and family life, is the Biblical scenario of what distinguishes a God-honouring family in all of its various relationships and responsibilities. It will only be as we individually fit into God's plan for the family that we shall know what it is to grow spiritually.

According to the statistics, one in three marriages ends in divorce and many more are only hanging together by a thread. Marriage is undeniably under attack in these days in which we live. Various experts have cynically and bitterly described their knowledge or experience of the married state. One such portrayed it as the 'peaceful co-existence of two nervous systems' while a marriage guidance counsellor after many years of trying to counsel couples with marriage problems said that 'marriage appeared to be a school of experience where husband and wife are clashmates.' The sad comment of one divorcee, however, reflecting the trauma of her experience was, 'Marriage is the world's most expensive way of discovering your faults.'

In spite of such negative comments, I want to underline that marriage and family life are divine institutions. They are not the product of man's innovation or the result of a long evolutionary process. Right at the beginning of creation God said, 'It is not good for the man to be alone: I will make a helper suitable for him...' For this reason a man will leave his father and mother and be united to his wife (Gen.2:18-24).

It was Matthew Henry who said:

God did not take the bone from Adam's foot that the woman might be beneath him. Nor did he take it from his head the she might be above him. He took it from his side that she might be equal to him; from underneath his arm that she might be protected by him; and near his heart that she might be loved by him.

What he was trying to say is that God is a romantic!

When we come to the New Testament we discover that God gives instructions to both husbands and wives in the context of the marriage relationship. Wives are told to 'submit to your husbands as to the Lord' and husbands are reminded to 'love your wives, just as Christ loved the church and gave himself up for her' (Eph 5:22,25).

Notice the emphasis that Paul places on the Lord. 'Wives submit ... as to the Lord,' and 'husbands love ... as Christ loved.' If you leave the Lord out of your marriage relationship then you will have problems. A successful marriage always involves a triangle: a man, a woman, and God. Paul writing to Titus even went so far as to say, 'Train the younger women to love their husbands and children' (Titus 2:4). There is to be mutual dependence between husband and wife, with a love that gives, but with the husband as the head of the home. Any reversal of God's order only causes problems and hinders spiritual growth. As George Duncan so aptly put it, 'The woman that rules the roost is on the wrong perch.'

One of the great blessings in any marriage is the arrival of children. They are God's gift to us as parents: 'Sons are a heritage from the Lord, children a reward from him' (Psalm 127:3). Someone has described a boy as 'nature's answer to the false belief that there is no such thing as perpetual motion. A boy can swim like a fish, run like a deer, climb like a squirrel, bellow like a bull, eat like a pig, or act like a mule. A boy is a piece of skin stretched over an appetite. He is a growing child of superlative promise, to be fed, watered and kept warm. He is a joy, a periodic nuisance, the problem of our time, but God's gift to you ...' I am sure that the same could be said of some girls as well. Children are a reward from him.

But our children will not just automatically go in the right direction. We do need to train them in the ways of God. The Duke of Wellington once said that, 'If you train children apart from religion, you will only make them clever devils.' And maybe this is one of the major reasons why there are so many problems among our youth population. Christian instruction and Biblical morality have been largely left out of their education and we are reaping the consequences. If we want to see spiritual growth in our children then we must lay the right foundation in their lives and the earlier we do that, the better it will be for them.

The New Testament puts the major responsisibility for spiritual training upon fathers: 'Fathers, do not exasperate your children; instead, bring them up in the training and instruction of the Lord' (Eph.6:4). It is obvious from life and experience that the influence of a godly mother is also invaluable. It is still true even today, that the 'hand that rocks the cradle will rule the world.' Dr. Jowett stated that 'where there is really a great man there was first a great mother.' Abraham Lincoln said, 'I remember my mother's prayers, they have always been with me.' George Herbert, the godly poet, considered that 'the influence of a good mother is worth more that a thousand schoolteachers.' This was also the opinion of Augustine who humbly gave thanks saying, 'If I am your child, O God, it is because you gave me such a mother.' Both father and mother can have a tremendous input into the spiritual awareness, commitment and growth of their children.

Parents are of course to provide for their children, to love them and train them. Solomon in the book of Proverbs said, 'Train a child in the way he should go, and when he is old he will not turn from it' (22:6). But parents are also to correct their children. The very first form of government with which a child comes in contact is in the home, so it is important that such government is a good one. Once again, Solomon gives good advice:

He who spares the rod hates his son, but he who loves him is careful to discipline him.

Discipline your son, for in that there is hope.

Do not withold discipline from a child; if you punish him with a rod, he will not die. Punish him with the rod and save his soul from death. (Prov.13:24; 19:18; 23:13,14).

Plato could have taught much to our juvenile courts to-day, for in his days physical punishment for crime was often handed out on the spot.

But possibly our greatest responsibility as parents is to recognise that we are stewards of our children. They are given to us on trust from God and one day we shall have to give account of our stewardship to God. It is not just up to them what they believe.

We must also never forget that children need a home as distinct from just a house. While their new home was being built, a doctor and his family had to live for a few months in a local hotel. One day a friend called to see the family and happened to say that it was a great pity that they did not have a home of their own. The youngest daughter quickly corrected the visitor and said with a wisdom beyond her years, 'But we do have a home, we just don't have a house to put it in to!' A home is the atmosphere and not just the bricks and mortar, so make sure that you promote a loving atmosphere for your children.

On the other side of the coin, children have their responsibilities to their parents: they are to give their attention to the teaching of their parents:

Listen, my son, to your father's instruction and do not forsake your mother's teaching (Prov. 1: 8,9).

Children, obey your parents in the Lord for this is right (Eph.6:1).

So here is God's picture and plan for a happy, harmonious family life where there is security, joy, peace and mutual love and fellowship. Anything less than adherence to God's blueprint as revealed in the Bible will be a stumbling block to Christian growth. Be determined that you will play your part in the spiritual growth of your family.

8
THE STEWARD

One of the great pictures of a Christian given to us in the New Testament is that of a steward. At least half of the parables that Jesus told were connected with stewardship. In the days in which Jesus lived, the steward of an Eastern household was second in authority to his master and had tremendous responsibilities.

But what do we mean by stewardship, and how does it apply to us today as Christians? A steward is 'one who manages another's property or financial affairs as the agent of the owner.' Or to put it another way: 'A steward is one who owns nothing, yet is responsible for everything.' As God's stewards we have had entrusted to us a number of priceless possessions, and all of these we only have on trust and we will, one day, be answerable to God for the way we use them. If you want to grow as a Christian then be determined to be a faithful steward of what he has entrusted to you. Stewardship basically covers all areas of life, and Christian growth depends largely upon how we fulfil our stewardship in these areas.

Stewardship - your faculties.

This involves your personality and the medium for expressing that personality - your body. Paul gives to us some very important teaching about the stewardship of our bodies when he writes, 'Do you not know that your body is a temple of the Holy Spirit, who is in you, whom you have received from God? You are not your own; you were bought at a price. Therefore honour God with your body' (1 Cor.6:19,20). The first and most important thing that you must understand is that your body belongs to God, and it is only when you recognise this fact, that you can begin to become a good steward.

Paul reminds us that 'the body is not meant for sexual immorality, but for the Lord, and the Lord for the body' (1Cor.6:13) He realised just how important was the stewardship of his own body in this respect, that he wrote, 'I beat my body and make it my slave so that after I have preached to others, I myself will not be disqualified for the prize' (1 Cor.9:27).

If you turn in your Bible to the first few verses of Romans 12 you will discover that the secret of successful stewardship of your body is realised when you 'offer your body as a living sacrifice, holy and pleasing to God - this is your spiritual act of worship.' A Christian must present all his faculties to God. He is to have a mind through which Christ thinks; a heart through which Christ loves; a voice through which Christ speaks; and a hand through which Christ helps.

Stewardship - your use of time

Time is one of God's great gifts and we are answerable to God for the way in which we use or misuse it. Thomas Edison once said, 'Time is the most valuable thing in the world' and it was Benjamin Franklin who commented, 'Do not squander time, for it is the stuff of which life is made.' But how often do we say when faced with some task or responsibility, 'If only I had the time.' The fact of the matter is that each of us has all the time available - twenty-four hours a day! It is the right management and use of the time that God has given to us that is so important. For God's gift of time is not a commodity that can be put into the bank and then drawn out and used on some future occasion. His gift of time must be invested hour by hour, or else it is gone forever.

There is a Greek legend which depicts opportunity and time as an old man with a long forelock of hair, but with his head perfectly bald at the back. He could be grasped by this forelock as he approached, but once past he could not be caught at all. Frederick Faber clearly understood this fleeting nature of opportunity and valued it as God-given. He said,'The surest method of arriving at a knowledge of God's eternal purpose about us is to be found in the right use of the present moment. Each hour comes with some little faggot of God's will fastened upon its back.'

Jesus too expressed the urgency of working according to God's time-scale and using the alloted period for achieving God's purpose: 'As long as it is day, we must do the work of him who sent me. Night is coming, when no-one can work' (John 9: 4). If this was true of Jesus, how much more is it true of us? Time is the coin of your life. It is the only coin you have, and only you can determine how it will be spent. Be careful lest you let other people spend it for you. A planned day is the secret of the successful stewardship of your time. Recognise that each day is a gift from God, given to you on trust.

If you are to be serious therefore in your stewardship you must be prepared to be careful in your use of time and look for God's will in the opportunities presented to you. Dr. Campbell Morgan was not alone in seeing this detailed care reflecting on our Christian lives as a whole: 'Let the year be given to God in its every moment! The year is made up of minutes: let these be watched as having been dedicated to God! It is in the sanctification of the small that the hallowing of the large is secure.'

Stewardship - our possessions

Before we look at some practical applications of the stewardship of our possessions, there are some important principles to underline.

You belong to God. 'You are not your own; you were bought at a price' (1Cor.6:19) - and that price says the apostle Peter was 'the precious blood of Christ' (1 Peter 1:19). When you came to Christ in response to his call, you received a new life and so now you are both completely dependent upon him and completely responsible to him. 'You are not your own.'

All possessions are held on trust. 'What do you have that you did not receive?' (1Cor.4:7). James in his epistle reminds us that 'every good and perfect gift is from above' (James 1:17). This not only refers to material possessions, but also to physical ability, intellect, emotions, and spiritual gifts. The danger so often is that exclusive use of that which does not belong to us often creates the illusion of ownership. If this illusion becomes a delusion and you act as you please with God's gifts, then you become a bad steward.

This life is a training period. It is only important in relation to the life to come. Jesus said, 'Do not store up for yourselves treasures on earth ... but store up for yourselves treasures in heaven' (Matt. 6:19,20). He also said, 'But seek first his kingdom and his righteousness, and all these things will be given to you as well' (Matt.6:33). Unless you see this life in the light of the next, your values will become distorted. To be good stewards, a godly perspective is required.

An account will be drawn up. How clearly this is illustrated in the classic parable that Jesus told in the story of the distribution of various talents by the master of the household to his stewards, and the command to put the talents to work: 'After a long time the master of those servants returned and settled accounts with them' (Matt.25:19). In other words they were all called to give an account of their stewardship - and so shall we be.

Giving to God

Having looked at some of the principles involved, let us move on and see what our attitudes to stewardship should be. Sadly, the attitudes to stewardship are very varied amongst Christians, and range from defiant neglect, haphazard emotive giving, through to the careful observance of New Testament standards of giving to God.

First of all, the Bible states quite clearly that giving is a duty as far as our own family is concerned: 'If any-one does not provide for his relatives, and especially for his immediate family, he has denied the faith and is worse than an unbeliever' (1 Tim.5:8). If you are a young person living at home, earning a good wage or salary and you don't give your parents a reasonable amount to keep you, then you are being a poor steward. Paul, in the same chapter, goes on to talk about our responsibility to give and support those of the Christian family who are engaged in Christian work: 'The elders who direct the affairs of the church well are worthy of double honour, especially those whose work is preaching and teaching' (1 Tim.5:17). In other words, the worker deserves his wages.

Giving is also an act of worship. Listen to what David says: 'Ascribe to the Lord the glory due to his name; bring an offering and come into his courts. Worship the Lord in the splendour of his holiness; tremble before him, all the earth' (Psalm 96:8,9). The offering at church is not half-time in the service when we pause for a chat with our neighbour, or look around to see who is there, or giggle about the mistakes that the church secretary made when giving out the notices. Giving to God is a very important part of our worship.

Giving to God should also be with a free spirit. 'Freely you have received,' said Jesus, so 'freely give' (Matt. 10:8). In fact, he went on to say that 'it is more blessed to give than to receive.' Giving should always be the overflow to love, for love always gives liberally. 'Give, and it will be given to you. A good measure, pressed down, shaken together and running over, will be poured into your lap. For with the measure you use, it will be measured to you' (Luke 6:38).

In the Old Testament, the prophet Malachi said: 'Bring the whole tithe into the storehouse that there may be food in my house. Test me in this,' says the Lord Almighty, 'and see if I will not throw open the floodgates of heaven and pour out so much blessing that you will not have room enough for it' (Mal. 3:10).

Faced with the generous gifts of God, David Livingstone was led to make this pledge: 'I will place no value on anything I have or may possess except in relation to the Kingdom of Christ. If anything will advance the interest of that Kingdom, it shall be given away or kept only as the giving or keeping of it shall most promote the glory of him to whom I owe all my hopes in time and eternity.' Such a free spirit in giving is rare, but it carries with it its own rich spiritual rewards.

Now there are four very important questions that we need to find an answer to, and they are as follows: How should we give? How much should we give? When should we give? Where should we give?

Moses gives us an important guideline when he says, 'No man should appear before the Lord empty handed. Each of you must bring a gift in proportion to the way the Lord your God has blessed you' (Deut. 16:16,17). God only expects you to give as you are able. Far more is expected of the rich man than the poor. Solomon reminds us how important it is to 'honour the Lord with you wealth, with the firstfruits of all your crops' (Prov.3:9).

Paul also gives careful instruction concerning these questions. Writing to the Corinthian church he teaches us: 'Each man should give what he has decided in his heart to give, not reluctantly or under compulsion, for God loves a cheerful giver' (2 Cor. 9:7). In his previous letter to these Christians he had also said, 'On the first day of every week, each one of you should set aside a sum of money in keeping with his income' (1Cor.16:2). Here are very clear directions as to how and when Christians should give.

From these Scriptures, two things come to light. Giving to God should be systematic and proportional - 'On the first day of the week,' and 'in keeping with his income.' Samuel Chadwick said: 'Unless a man cultivates a habit of systematic giving when he has not much to give, he will give little when he is rich.'

Now the question is, what should that proportion be? The Mosaic law of giving one tenth only affirmed an already existing law and principle; and that principle Abraham obviously recognised and obeyed because he paid tithes. It can certainly be said that the lowest standard of giving taught in the Bible is one tenth of a person's income, so the question to ask ourselves is, can we as Christians give less than this? And remember that the Bible speaks of tithes - and offerings! The tenth already belongs to God, and offerings should be added to this as an expression of our love to Christ.

As a Christian you have no idea what you are missing in terms of spiritual enrichment until you learn to give on God's terms, for let me remind you again that Jesus said, 'It is more blessed to give than to receive.' If as parents you give your children pocket money, then give it to them in multiples of ten pence so that they can easily learn to tithe from an early age. God's blessing comes to those who recognise their responsibility in terms of the stewardship of their money.

But where should you give your money? Certainly you have a financial responsibility to your own local church, its upkeep, ministry and outreach. Possibly the largest part of your regular giving should be to and through your local church if it is functioning in a Biblical way. However, don't restrict your giving to the local church but take a practical and financial interest in home and overseas missions. Why not reg-ularly support an evangelist or a missionary for you will pray more meaningfully for Christian work when you also support it financially?

If your salary is such that you pay income tax, then it is possible to give under what is called a 'Deed of Covenant'. Your regular gift is then increased in value as far as the church or missionary society is concerned because they can reclaim the tax you have paid on that amount of your income. Any church or missionary society secretary or treasurer would gladly give you details of this scheme for wise stewardship.

There is no greater joy than giving to the Lord and his work. There are God-given rewards for faithful stewardship for it has been said that 'money, that most temporal of things, involves uncommon and eternal consequences.' There is actually no portion of our time that is *our* time, and the rest God's; there is no portion of money that is *our* money and the rest God's money. It is all his; he made it all, gives it all, and he has simply entrusted it to us for his service. Adolphe Monod put it like this: 'A servant has two purses, his master's and his own; but we have only one!' So how is your giving to God? Is it minimal, is it satisfactory, or is it an overflow of love?

Can I suggest to you a very practical exercise right now? Stop reading any further in this book and get pen and paper and write down a few facts and figures that at the end of the day might really surprise and challenge you.

First of all, make a note of what you spend each week on the extras such as sweets, magazines, entertainment, newspapers etc., and multiply the figure by 52 weeks in the year. Then add on the cost of cosmetics, aftershave, deodorants and perfumes. Then what about coffee and cakes when you are out in town, the visit to football or rugby and eating out for an evening? Add to all of this the money spent on the annual holiday including spending money, new clothes, TV, records, videos and cassettes. If you have made a reasonably accurate list of these things you will be surprised to see just how much you have spent on yourself, your family and your friends. Now, of course, none of these things are necessarily wrong or illegitimate for you as a Christian. But now list how much of your income has been given in a direct way to God during the same period? You might feel very ashamed when you make the comparison and see just how little you have actually given to God.

Many church and missionary organisations would not be in the financial stranglehold that they are now in if only we, as Christians, would give even a tithe of our income. Twenty working Christians earning only £140 per week and tithing would be able to give £280 every week to Christian work. If you move up the scale to a hundred Christians earning on average the same amount, then the tithe would produce £1,400 per week for the support of their church and the work of God overseas. Start giving to God and you will start growing as a Christian.

9
JOINING THE CHURCH

A former Archbishop of Canterbury was once asked on a television programme if he was a high or low churchman. His reply was illuminating for he said, 'I have a high opinion of the church.' Although I think that he evaded the question, in one sense he was right. Every Christian should have a high opinion of the church. By the church, I do not mean a building or a denomination, but the worldwide company of men, women and children who have received Jesus Christ as Saviour and Lord and who there-fore have already been brought into the church.

The word 'church' is always used in the Bible to describe people, never a building. The Greek word *ecclesia* which is translated 'church' over 115 times, always means 'a congregation' or 'a group of people' or 'those that have been called out.'

However, this word 'church' is presented in two different ways in the New Testament. Firstly, it is used of the universal church, or the total number of believers worldwide who have been called out by Christ through the Spirit. For example, it is the word used by Paul when he says, 'Now you are the body of Christ, and each one of you is a part of it. And in the church God has appointed first of all apostles, second prophets, third teachers ...' (1 Cor. 12:27,28) and again, 'His intent was that now, through the church, the manifold wisdom of God should be made known' (Eph.3:10).

Secondly, the word is used of the local church. Writing to the Romans Paul says, 'I commend to you our sister Phoebe, a servant of the church in Cenchrea' (Rom. 16:1); and it is obviously local churches that are referred to in the first three chapters of the book of Revelation.

Before Paul finally said farewell to the elders of the Ephesian church on his way to Jerusalem, he not only recounted to them his own ministry amongst them, but he also urged them to carry on the good work. In his exhortation he said, 'Keep watch over yourselves and all the flock of which the Holy Spirit has made you overseers. Be shepherds of the church of God, which he bought with his own blood' (Acts 20:28). The church of Jesus Christ is universal, but it has expressions all over the world in local churches.

The founder of the church

When Jesus said, 'I will build my church, and the gates of Hades will not overcome it' (Matt.16:18), the context of his statement was the confession of Peter, 'You are the Christ, the Son of the living God' (Matt.16:16). Jesus then said to Peter, 'This was not revealed to you by man, but by my Father in Heaven. And I tell you that you are Peter, and on this rock I will build my *church*' (Matt.16:17,18).

Roman Catholics interpret these verses as meaning that Jesus was saying that the church was to be built upon Peter and that he was to be the foundation of the church. As they also believe that Peter was the first Bishop of Rome, they therefore consider that the Roman Catholic Church is the only true church. But this was not what Jesus was teaching. Look at these verses again in your Bible because it is very important that you understand what Jesus actually said.

The Greek word for Peter which Jesus uses is *petros* which literally means 'a piece of rock.' But the Greek word for 'upon this rock' is *petra* - and that means 'a huge rock.' Peter had just confessed Jesus as 'the Christ, the Son of the living God,' when Jesus said to him, 'You are *petros* - a piece of rock, and on this *petra* - the huge rock - I will build my church.' Jesus was speaking about himself as the rock, the foundation stone.

This was certainly how the apostle Paul understood the meaning of *petra*. In writing to the Corinthian Christians and reminding them of

Israel's past history in the wilderness many centuries before, Paul said of their forefathers, 'They all ate the same spiritual food and drank... from the spiritual rock that accompanied them, and that rock was Christ' (1 Cor.10:4).

In fact, 'rock' is one of the Lord's titles in both Old and New Testaments: 'The Lord is my rock.' (Psalm 18:2) and 'for no- one can lay any foundation other than the one already laid, which is Jesus Christ' (1 Cor.3:11).

The future of the church

Jesus Christ is not only the founder and foundation of the church, he is also the architect and builder. He promises: 'I will build my church' (Matt16:18). Because it is his church, it belongs to him. We as members of his church can therefore rejoice in this glorious fact. Following on from his great statement about the foundation of the church Jesus teaches two things about the future of the church that are very important.

Firstly, the church will be invincible when attacked: 'The gates of Hades will not overcome it' (Matt. 16:18) The church of Jesus Christ has been assaulted right from its birth. Stephen, one of the deacons of the Jerusalem church during the early days, was brutally murdered as he gave testimony to Christ (Acts.7:57). General persecution against the church then broke out and 'all except the apostles were scattered.' In addition, 'Saul began to destroy the church. Going from house to house, he dragged off men and women and put them in prison' (Acts 8:1,2). It certainly looked as if the future of the church was hanging on a thread. Could it survive such antagonism?

Yes it could, and did. Immediately after the death of Stephen and the persecution by Saul we read that 'those who had been scattered, preached the word wherever they went' (Acts 8:4). Amongst those scattered was Philip, a colleague of the martyred Stephen. He went down to Samaria and preached Christ and thousands were converted and added to the church. From Samaria, God directed him to a desert road between Jerusalem and Gaza and there he met a high official of Ethiopia. Philip preached the gospel to him and saw him come to faith in Christ.

Saul, in persecuting the church, was determined to blot it out: 'Breathing out murderous threats against the Lord's disciples he went to the high priest and asked him for letters to the synagogue in Damascus, so that if he found any there who belonged to the Way, whether men or women, he might take them as prisoners to Jerusalem' (Acts 9:1,2). But on the way to carry out his diabolical plot, God met him in grace and mercy and opened his spiritual eyes to see the truth of Christ; Saul was converted. He subsequently went on to be the greatest evangelist and missionary pioneer that the church has ever known.

Secondly, the church will be invincible when on the attack. From a situation of apparent disaster and oblivion before the conversion of Saul we read that 'the church throughout Judea, Galilee and Samaria enjoyed a time of peace. It was strengthened and encouraged by the Holy Spirit, it grew in numbers, living in the fear of the Lord' (Acts 9:31). Yes, there was already ample evidence that the church was invincible and could attack the citadels of Satan and unbelief.

Church history from the first century to the twentieth gives further evidence of the certainty of that promise of Jesus to Peter. Through the Dark and Middle Ages when it faced severe persecution from Roman Catholicism and then during our lifetime being pressured by atheistic communism, the church has been refined and has emerged even stronger. 'I will build my church,' says Jesus, 'and the gates of Hades shall not prevail against it' (Matt. 16:18).

John, writing in the book of Revelation, depicts the end of time and the ultimate triumph of the church of Jesus Christ. He sees, in a vision, around the throne of God, a great company of the saved of the earth. He describes the One standing at the centre of the throne as a 'Lamb looking as if it had been slain' (Rev.5:6). Remember that John the Baptist described Jesus as 'the Lamb of God, who takes away the sin of the world' (John 1:29). It is of this 'Lamb' that John hears the hosts of heaven declaring:

> You are worthy to take the scroll and to open its seals, because you were slain, and with your blood you purchased men for God from every tribe and language and people and nation. You have made them to be a kingdom and priests to serve our God, and they will reign on the earth' (Rev.5:9,10).

How wonderful it is to know that the church is made up of people from all over the world.

So this is the church. It is universal and yet local. Jesus is the founder, and the guarantor of its future. You are already a member of the universal church if you are a Christian, but if you want to grow as a Christian, it is essential that you link up with and become a member of a local church. It will be in the context of a local church that you will find fellowship, get teaching and instruction, discover what gifts God has given to you, and also start to serve him.

Joining a church

But which church do you join? This is a very important question. It may not be a problem for you because possibly your parents or friends belong to a church and you have already attended it with them. If you were converted in a church which someone invited you to attend, then that is where you probably should go. Difficulties arise if you became a Christian when you were away from home, studying or working. If you had never attended church in your home town, you might not know where to start looking for one that would be helpful and in which you could grow.

If you did come to the Lord when away from home, then do ask the minister or leader of the church where you were converted if they could recommend a good church in your home locality. If he does not know of one personally then he can find out for you quickly. Whatever you do, don't expect to find the perfect church. It does not exist, and if it did and you joined it, then you would spoil it!

What is essential for you as a young Christian is to find a church which believes God's Word and preaches it faithfully. It is usually also helpful if you can find such a church within walking distance of your home. It is not always possible in today's world, but if it is, then there is no doubt that this is an advantage from the point of view of being a witness in the locality of your church.

The largest church is not always the best one for you, but for some it may be right. If there are several good churches in your area then visit them and pray and seek the Lord's guidance as to which he would have you join. If you are young, then see if it is a church with other young people. If you are married and have children, does the church have a thriving Sunday School or youth activities? The church you join will not only affect you, but also your family as well.

Whatever you do, don't become a spiritual gypsy and wander from church to church. Such travellers rarely develop spiritually and are usually a pain in the neck to the fellowship that they drop in on from time to time. Once you have found the right church for you, then as soon as possible become a member and start to play a full part in its worship and ministry.

What happens in the church?

Jesus gave two ordinances to the church: Baptism, and The Lord's Supper. They are both very important and should not be neglected.

In the New Testament baptism would always seem to have followed conversion. On the Day of Pentecost, after Peter preached his first evangelistic message, there was great conviction in the hearts of his hearers. Luke who records what happened wrote: 'When the people heard this, they were cut to the heart and said to Peter and the other apostles, "Brothers, what shall we do?" Peter replied, "Repent and be baptised"' (Acts 2:38).

The Ethiopian Chancellor of the Exchequer after he was converted under the preaching of Philip requested baptism (Acts9:38).

When Saul was converted en route to Damascus, Ananias was sent by God to counsel him. Of this meeting we read, 'Immediately, something like scales fell from Saul's eyes, and he could see again. He got up and was baptised' (Acts 9:18).

Peter was used by God to open the door of faith to the Gentiles. When the heart of the Roman centurion was opened to the gospel, Peter said, ' "Can anyone keep these people from being baptised with water? They have received the Holy Spirit just as we have." So he ordered that they be baptised in the name of Jesus Christ' (Acts 10:47).

Depending on the church you become a member of you will discover that there are basically two methods of baptism and they signify different understandings of baptism. One is by immersion where the person being baptised goes down into the water and the second method is by effusion which means that water is poured on the head of the person.

The Lord's Supper

Shortly before Jesus was betrayed by Judas, he called his disciples together and instituted what we now call the Lord's Supper or Holy Communion. The original event is recorded for us in both the Gospels of Matthew and Luke:

> He took bread, gave thanks and broke it, and gave it to them saying, 'This is my body given for you; do this in rememberance of me.' In the same way, after the supper he took the cup saying, 'This cup is the new covenant in my blood, which is poured out for you' (Luke 22: 19,20).

It was a very vivid visual aid to demonstrate what he was shortly going to be doing. Jesus was going to go to the cross and bear in his body our sin, and shed his blood as an atonement for that sin.

Paul, writing to the Corinthians makes it quite clear that a re-enactment or a celebration of this Supper is what the Lord desires us to participate in. Paul says:

> For I received from the Lord what I also passed

on to you: The Lord Jesus, on the night he was betrayed, took bread, and when he had given thanks, he broke it and said, 'This is my body, which is broken for you; do this in remembrance of me.' In the same way, after supper he took the cup saying, 'This cup is the new covenant in my blood; do this, whenever you drink it, in remembrance of me.' For whenever you eat this bread and drink this cup, you proclaim the Lord's death until he comes (1 Cor. 11:23-26).

Participation in the Lord's Supper is the privilege of all true believers, so do respond to the Lord's invitation and come and remember what he did for you. It is an exclusive supper; only the Lord's people are invited to it. They should remember as they enjoy this meal that it is both a free and an expensive supper. It is without a fee because Jesus has paid the price himself: 'For you know that it was not with perishable things such as silver or gold that you were redeemed ... but with the precious blood of Christ' (1 Peter 1:18,19).

So how should we prepare ourselves as we come to the Lord's Supper? First of all, the Bible tells us that 'every one ought to examine themselves before we eat of the bread and drink of the cup' (1 Cor.11:28). This is not in order to disqualify ourselves, but rather to encourage us to keep short accounts with God. If there is unconfessed sin then remember the promise of God: 'If we confess our sins, he is faithful and just and will forgive us our sins and purify us from all unrighteousness' (1John 1:9). We, of course, also have the assurance of God's forgiveness, because every time we come to the Lord's Table we look back to Calvary where we see the Lamb of God, taking away the sin of the world (John 1:29).

But the Lord's Table is not only for us to look back and remember the sorrow and suffering of the Lord Jesus Christ on our behalf. We also rejoice that he is risen, ascended and glorified. This is Jesus - the Conquerer whom we meet at his table; a victorious Saviour.

The Lord's Table is also a sharing experience because we come in fellowship with other Christians. As we take the bread and the wine we do so in recognition that as we belong to Christ, we also belong to each other, members of the household of faith.

Lastly, what is so exciting about coming to the Lord's Supper is that we are testifying to our belief and confidence that the Lord Jesus who suffered and died for us, who rose again and ascended into heaven, is to come again. On Ascension Day as Jesus was received up into heaven, two angels appeared to those wondering disciples and said: 'This same Jesus, who has been taken from you into heaven, will come back in the same way you have seen him go into heaven' (Acts 1:11). Paul confirms: 'For whenever you eat this bread and drink this cup, you proclaim the Lord's death until he comes' (1 Cor. 11:26).

Preparation for worship

Worship does not start in church once you arrive, but it begins with an attitude of heart and mind that is not switched on or off according to the day of the week or any building that you may enter. The first commandment of all is to 'Worship the Lord your God, and serve him only' (Matt. 4:10). God is concerned that you learn to worship him before you start to work for him. Worshippers always make the best workers. But of one thing you can be sure and that is that the Devil, the world and the flesh will all join forces to seek to prevent you from worshipping God.

The word for worship used most commonly in the New Testament is *proskuneo* and it means to do reverence, do homage or to adore. It is, for example, the word of the wise men who came to question King Herod: 'Where is the one who has been born king of the Jews?... We have come to worship him' (Matt. 2:2). Later when they found the One they had been searching for we read: 'On coming to the house, they saw the child with his mother Mary, and they bowed down and worshipped him (Matt.2:11). Jesus himself used this same word when he spoke to the woman of Samaria: 'God is spirit, and his worshippers must worship in spirit and in truth' (John 4:24).

But it is the way in which the word 'worship' is first used in the Bible which helps us understand what is involved. In Genesis 22 we read the story of Abraham being told by God to go to Mount Moriah and offer his son as a sacrifice. (If you want to stop and read the story for yourself at this point it might be helpful.)

Notice that Abraham went to worship because God told him to: 'God said...' (Gen.22:1). Our worship of God must always be guided by the Word of God. We live in an age when there are those who tell us that we can worship God in all kinds of ways and particularly with the arts. Dance, drama and even rock music are suggested as being suitable vehicles for expressing our worship to God. But God certainly has not said so and some art forms that may be a perfectly acceptable form of relaxation and entertainment are certainly not acceptable mediums for the worship of the holy God. (Some art forms are not even suitable for our relaxation and pleasure. All must be tested by the standards of the Word of God.) God has to be worshipped in truth as well as in spirit.

It is also important to notice that worship springs from faith in God and his Word and that faith is expressed in obedience to its teachings. As soon as God spoke to Abraham, he believed and obeyed. You will not be able to worship unless you listen to God in his Word and then when he does speak to you, obey. Obedience is part of worship.

In addition, worship always involves a deliberate separation from the things that have occupied your attention, legitimate though they may be, and a concentration of your mind upon the things of God. Abraham said to the young men who had accompanied him and Isaac on their journey to Mount Moriah, 'Stay *here* with the donkey, while I and the boy go over *there*. We will worship and then we will come back to you' (Gen. 22:5).

From this incident in Abraham's life we will also realize that true worship is costly. In Abraham's case it meant presenting his dearly beloved son unreservedly to God. When God spoke to Abraham he reminded him of these facts, 'Take your son, your only son Isaac whom you love.'

Yet the consequence of truly worshipping God is always blessing. When Abraham returned from the mountain, God spoke to him and said,

'Because you have done this and have not with-held your son, your only son, I will surely bless you and make your descendants as numerous as the stars in the sky and as the sand on the seashore ... through your offspring all nations on earth will be blessed because you have obeyed me' (Gen.22:16,17,18).

Worship, therefore, involves obedience; it is the fruit of faith; it is costly; it is deliberate; and it always results in blessing. Be determined as a young Christian that you are not going to miss out on being a worshipper of God. As you learn to worship so you will start to grow.

Before you set out for church next Sunday, seek to prepare your heart for worship. Do not fill your mind with the events of the past week or with the programme for the next week. Don't make Sunday just a day for meeting friends and passing on information. Sunday is the Lord's Day, so keep him uppermost in your thoughts. Of course, Sunday is a day to meet with fellow Christians. But in it all, remember the words of the Lord Jesus Christ, your Saviour: 'Worship the Lord your God and serve him only.'

Responsibilities in your local church
Once you have become a member of a local church, be present as often as possible at the services, not

only on a Sunday, but also during the week at the prayer and Bible study meetings.

Being a member of a local church brings you into contact with other Christians of different ages and backgrounds and also at varying levels of Christian experience. It is similar to being brought into a family and in a good family it is not all one-way communication and service. Be a good learner. Older Christians have picked up a lot of valuable experience. If they share some of that experience with you, treat it as a bonus and learn from it.

God has not just called you into the fellowship of a local church for your enjoyment. It is also for you to be in his employment, but enjoyable it most certainly is. There is not a greater joy that the joy of serving God. Ask the Lord first of all to make clear to you what gift or gifts he has given you. Can you easily relate to children? Then there might be a job for you in the Sunday School. Do you get on well with teenagers and are personal relationships your strong point? Are you a good listener, and do you get on well with old people? Do you have practical skills or administrative abilities? Discover what your gift is if you are not already aware of it, and ask the minister or leaders of your church what there is for you to be involved in as service to the Lord.

You cannot be a 'Robinson Crusoe, Desert Island - who goes it alone' Christian. If you want to grow as a Christian, you need the fellowship and help of a local church. So go and join one and get working for God.

10

WITNESSING FOR CHRIST

After his resurrection Jesus appeared to the disciples and gave to them the great commission.

> All authority in heaven and on earth has been given to me. Therefore go and make disciples of all nations (Matt.28:18,19).

> Go into all the world and preach the good news to all creation (Mark 16:15).

> But you will receive power when the Holy Spirit comes on you; and you will be my witness in Jerusalem, and in all Judea and Samaria, and to the ends of the earth (Acts 1:8).

Jesus could not have put more plainly our responsibility as Christians to take the gospel to others. It was not just a word for those select disciples but for all of members of the church of Jesus Christ. Sadly there seem to be three kinds of church members today: effective, ineffective and defective. If you do not as a Christian share your faith with others, then you will be numbered amongst the defective and you will not grow as a Christian.

So how can you be an effective witness? Firstly, all you need to know about the faith is found in the Bible. Here is yet another reason why you should read it regularly and systematically. As you continue reading you will speedily discover that your faith centres in a person, Jesus Christ. He gives to you pardon, peace, power and his presence in your life.

You must also be aware that it is a personal faith you are to share and you cannot share or bear witness to what you do not possess. Let me repeat again how important it is that you are certain that you are converted to Jesus Christ. Without such an experience, all of your efforts will be in vain. C.H. Spurgeon once said, 'God will not use dead tools to work living miracles.' If you are going to help someone else, you must first of all have been converted.

Then, of course, you can only really share your faith if you are a dedicated Christian. Your life must be a good advertisement for the gospel. Verbal presentation, however logical, will always fall flat, unless it is supplemented by the demonstration of a changed life. Edward Dayton said, 'The church doesn't need a message that is relevant to the world. It needs Christians who are relevant to the message.' David the Psalmist expressed this truth very forcibly when he wrote: 'Create in me a pure heart, O God... then I will teach transgressors your ways, and sinners will turn back to you' (Psalm 51: 10,13).

Salt and light

In the Sermon on the Mount, Jesus gave two very interesting descriptions of what Christian effect and witness in the world is to be:

> You are the salt of the earth. But if the salt loses its saltiness, how can it be made salty again? It is no longer good for anything except to be thrown out and trampled by men. You are the light of the world. A city on a hill cannot be hidden (Matt.5:13,14).

Salt and light are the two ways in which Jesus described Christians, and in so doing he was emphasising to us, not our attitude to the world, but rather our influence in the world.

Salt has no substitute because it is unique. It is distinct. You do not compare salt with anything but rather other things are compared to it. We sometimes say of food, 'Isn't it salty!' This is the sort of influence that Jesus wants you to have in the world in which you live. He wants you to have an influence for which there is no substitute.

Another characteristic of salt is that it does its work in secret. The influence of salt is subtle. Small in quantity, it can influence and permeate the whole. Though you may not see that it has been added to the water in which you cook the vegetables, it can be tasted. You may feel small and insignificant as a Christian and unable to be much of a witness in your situation. But, remember, you are 'salt' and a small amount can effect a much larger area than you could possibly imagine.

Many other functions are also fulfilled by salt. Salt when added is a preservative because it combats decay. It gives flavour and it can have a healing effect because it has antiseptic properties. You are to have a similar effect as by your life's witness you combat decay, and give flavour and bring healing. Jesus said, 'You are the salt of the earth.'

Light is very different from salt in what it does. Salt does its work in what you might describe as an undercover way. But light is very open and positive. It shines publicly and openly. Light is descriptive of the character of God. In the Old Testament we read: 'For with you is the fountain of life; in your light we see light' (Psalm 36:9). In the New Testament, Paul wrote: 'For you were once darkness, but now you are light in the Lord' (Eph.5:8).

As Christians we are possessors of the light because Jesus who is the Light of the world lives and dwells within us. We possess the light in order that we might transmit it to others. Paul says that we are to 'shine like stars in the universe' (Phil.2:15).

When Latimer and Ridley were about to be burnt at the stake in Oxford, Latimer turned to Ridley and said, 'Play the man, Ridley, and we shall light such a candle this day by God's grace in England as I trust shall never be put out.' You may never be called to provide such a light as they did in their martyrdom, but you are equally called to be light in a dark world.

The operative word is GO

As you read through the Gospels you will discover a word that Jesus used to people who came to him for salvation and forgiveness - 'Go'. To the woman taken in adultery, Jesus said, 'Go now and leave your life of sin' (John 8:11). 'Go, wash in the pool of Siloam' (John 9:7) was the command of Jesus to the blind man after he had anointed his eyes. To the rich young ruler it was, 'Go, sell everything you have' (Mark 10:21). The father's word to his son because of their relationship was,

'Go and work today in the vineyard' (Matt.21:28). Philip the evangelist heard the voice of the Lord saying to him, 'Go to that chariot and stay near it' (Acts 8:29). It is this divine imperative that comes in the great commission as Jesus says, 'Go into all the world and preach the good news to all creation' (Mark 16:15).

If you know that you are a Christian and belong to Christ because you have believed the gospel, then God wants you to do something about sharing the gospel with others who as yet have never heard.

Hints on how to give away your faith
Giving away your faith always involves *prayer*. Pray specifically for friends and relatives to come to know your Saviour. Keep a card ready in your Bible on which are listed their names and this will help you to remember them regularly in your prayers.

Give the gospel away *compassionately*, with real love and concern for people with real needs, problems and longings. The people you witness to are not just 'lost souls'.

Give it away *personally* in conversation. It is still true that personal sharing of the faith on a one to one basis and between friends is by far the most effective form of evangelism.

Give it away *spiritually*. Witnessing in the Acts of the Apostles was only effective in the power of the Holy Spirit and it is still the only way today.

Give it away *collectively*. Join in the witness of your Youth Fellowship, School or College Christian Union or Works Fellowship, and, of course, make sure that you take part in the evangelistic outreach of your own local church.

Give it away *practically* by your good works. Paul said that 'we are created in Christ Jesus to do good works' (Eph.2:10). Jesus told his disciples: 'Let your light shine before men, that they may see your good deeds and praise your Father in heaven' (Matt.5:16).

Aim to give your faith away in terms of living, speaking of it, demonstrating it practically and, if need be, sometimes even suffering for it. Witnessing for Christ will help you to grow as a Christian.

Missionary work - Divine imperative or an optional extra?

One of the great tragedies in many of our contemporary churches is that few Christians accept any responsibility for the missionary task of taking the gospel overseas and into a cross-cultural situation. You would think by the attendance at most missionary meetings that mission was an optional extra instead of a Divine imperative.

When Jesus gave us the great commission to 'go into all the world and preach the Good News to all creation' he was not giving us a suggestion. Jesus did not give us an option, it was an order. A solemn obligation is laid upon us because he commands us to go. It is of no use singing over and over again, 'Majesty, worship his Majesty,' if we are not being obedient servants of His Majesty. When God calls, you are both privileged and obliged to answer with obedience and to start by making yourself available to God.

Disobedience to the Lord's command deprives countless thousands of the opportunity to hear the gospel for even the first time. There may be a place for the teaching of the illiterate, the sheltering of the refugee and the healing of the sick. But the task which our Lord Jesus Christ has called us to engage in is to preach the gospel. It was Canon Patterson, an Anglican clergyman, who said, 'I wonder which shows more of the loving kindness of the Lord. His patience with those that won't come, or a church that won't go.'

The early disciples certainly took Jesus at his word and went into the world of their day to do exactly what Jesus had told them to do. In fact, the only one of the twelve who did not become a missionary became a traitor! David Livingstone said, 'God had only one Son, and he was a missionary.'

On the Day of Pentecost, the first preaching of the Christian gospel was a missionary presentation to various groups of people present in Jerusalem for the feast, from many parts of the world. Amongst those listening to Peter's sermon were, 'Parthians, Medes and Elamites, residents of Mesopotamia, Judea and Cappadocia ... and the parts of Libya ... visitors from Rome ... Cretans and Arabs...' (Acts 2:9,11). The church was born in a missionary context.

As you continue to read the Acts of the Apostles you will find many other examples of this procedure. In Acts 8 when the church in Jerusalem began to be persecuted, Philip went to Samaria and took the gospel to this group of people. Later in the same chapter we find him leaving all that was happening in Samaria to go down to a desert road, this time to share the gospel with the Ethiopian whom we mentioned earlier. Through him, the gospel was first taken to Ethiopia.

Peter, as an ardent Jew found himself called of God to take the gospel to a Roman centurion in Caesarea (Acts 10&11). In the subsequent chapter we find that the gospel is being taken by Christian men from Cyprus and Cyrene to Greeks living in

Antioch. It sounds confusing but it was under God's command!

Similarly, Paul and Barnabas were commissioned by the church in Antioch to take the Christian message to other lands, and so they visited Cyprus and Antioch in Pisidia. Timothy and Silas joined Paul for visits to Thessalonica and Philippi, and later Paul travelled to Athens, Corinth and Ephesus. The whole of the Acts of the Apostles is a missionary story.

The church of Jesus Christ has only been established where it is in the world today because Christian men and women down through the centuries have realised that it is the responsibility of believers in every generation to see that the gospel is proclaimed to the world.

Missionary involvement is the responsibility of every Christian in one way or another. That is why it is so important at the beginning of your Christian life to ask God what part you should have in spreading the gospel to people who have not heard it. In the light of a soaring world population, the resurgence of many eastern religions and the alarming number of doors closing due to the advance of Islam and other militant religious groups, how important it is that the missionary task of the church should be taken up by all true believers in the Lord Jesus Christ.

Every person without Christ is a mission field, and every person with Christ is a missionary. We cannot bring the whole world to Christ, but we must bring Christ to the whole world. With this in mind, where do you begin as individuals to seek to discover what God might want you to do?

Step by step guide to mission

Try to have an intelligent understanding of the missionary situation in the world today. One thing is certain: you will never have a real heart concern for missionary work unless you know what is happening in at least some parts of the world. Buy yourself a map of the world or an atlas and find out as much as possible about the various continents and countries as far as the Christian church is concerned. Read missionary books when they appear on your church bookstall or as you see them in your Christian bookshop. Subscribe to at least one missionary magazine and take an interest in at least one missionary. Write to him or her regularly. Ask questions about their work, the joy, the problems and difficulties they experience. Ask about the religion and culture of the area they are working in. Read newspaper reports and listen to news bulletins when there is news of the country your missionaries are working in.

Pray regularly and systematically for missionary work and for your specific missionaries and read missionary prayer letters. If you have decided as suggested in the chapter on prayer to have a personal prayer note book, then list items for prayer which concern the missionaries that you know. One book that I have found invaluable in this connection is called *Operation World,* a daily guide to praying for the world. It is written by Patrick Johnstone and it is published by STL Books and WEC Publications. Any Christian bookshop will get it for you if they do not already stock it. All the countries of the world are listed in alphabetical order and there are details of the Christian situation in each country; what missionary input there is and what still needs to be done. You can read the book just for information on the world scene, or better still use it to systematically pray for the world. Many Christians may never reach the mission field on their feet, but all of God's children can reach it on their knees.

Give financially to missionary work in a regular way, either through your church missionary fund if it has one, or directly to a missionary society or individual missionary that you have begun to pray for. Give in a way that entails sacrifice, and not just because the missionary you have been listening to happens to be a good speaker and you feel emotionally stirred. (Some missionaries are poor public speakers, but do a great work on the mission field.)

Make sure that you support missionary meetings arranged at your local church and in your locality. No missionary will be encouraged to continue with the work God has called him to if he sees rows of empty seats in the church where he is speaking.

Every Christian should seriously consider the claims of Christ upon their lives for missionary service and there are a number of reasons why you should consider such a possibility.

First of all, because you are a child of God you have the special privilege of taking the gospel to people who have never heard about Jesus. It ought not to be a duty but a delight. Also consider it because now that you are a Christian you have been brought into the church of Jesus Christ, and mission is the responsibility of the church.

An added responsibility is that God has given to us in our country a great Christian heritage and background. We have had centuries of Christian teaching, literature and freedom. When much has been given then much is expected of us by God:

From everyone who has been given much, much will be demanded; and from the one who has been entrusted with much, much more will be asked (Luke 12:48).

Lastly, you have the responsibility because God has provided you with the spiritual resources that we need to accomplish the task - he has given the Spirit. Jesus promised: 'You will receive power when the Holy Spirit comes on you' (Acts 1:8).

Years after his conversion the apostle Paul described how God had commanded him to go the Gentiles, and he added, 'I was not disobedient to the heavenly vision.' We are surely all grateful that he was not! This generation living in today's world are our responsibility - they are not the responsibility of Paul.

The work that our Lord Jesus came to accomplish and has handed on to us cannot be done by remote control, but only by getting involved. While it is absolutely true that God alone, in his sovereign grace, gives the increase, yet he does involve some in planting, others in watering, and all with the same objective of an abundant harvest. Jesus called his disciples to him for training so that they might be eventually sent out to serve him. His call to commitment is certainly clear, and his great commission still awaits fulfilment. How sad it is when so few answer that call with obedience.

Before he died tragically in a plane crash, Keith Green wrote a very challenging song:

Jesus commands us to go;
It should be the exception if we stay,
It's no wonder we're moving so slow,
When God's children refuse to obey.

Mission is not an optional extra, it is a divine imperative. If you want to grow in the Christian life then you cannot afford to ignore the challenge of the great commission of the Lord Jesus.

11

THE MINISTRY OF THE HOLY SPIRIT

Having looked briefly at some of the things that are essential for spiritual growth, possibly you are beginning to feel that such growth for you is going to be very difficult, maybe well nigh impossible, for you know your own heart too well. God, however, has not left you alone, because the most priceless possession that God has given to you for the advancement of your Christian life and its steady day by day growth is the Holy Spirit. In this last chapter I want to look at what the Bible says about our relationship with the Holy Spirit, and what he can increasingly become to us along the pathway of Christian growth.

There is a great deal of misconception and confusion about the Holy Spirit, so it is important before we begin to look at our relationship with him that we see something of who he is. Is the Holy Spirit just an influence or a power, or is he a person? The Bible leaves us in no doubt at all for it clearly teaches that the Holy Spirit is a person. Speaking to his disciples Jesus said of the Holy Spirit:

I will ask the Father, and he will give you another Counsellor to be with you for ever - the Spirit of truth. The world cannot accept him, because it neither sees him nor knows him. But you know him, for he lives with you and will be in you (John 14:16,17).

I have much more to say to you, more than you can now bear. But when he, the Spirit of truth comes, he will guide you into all truth (John 16:12,13).

Notice how the personal pronoun is used as Jesus outlines some of the activities of the Holy Spirit.

When Peter had the vision which is recorded for us in Acts 10, and was still thinking about it, 'the Spirit said to him, "Simon, three men are looking for you. So get up and go downstairs. Do not hesitate to go with them, for I have sent them"' (Acts 10:19,20). Notice that the Holy Spirit speaks, and only a person can speak.

Ananias and Sapphira, we are told in Acts 5, 'lied to the Holy Spirit'; Paul reminds us that the Holy Spirit possesses intelligence when he says the 'Spirit searches all things' (1 Cor. 2:10). Can you lie to an influence, or does such an influence have intelligence? Speaking about the distribution of spiritual gifts Paul tells us that 'all these are the work of one and the same Spirit, and he gives them to each one, just as he determines' (1 Cor. 12:11).

We also discover as we read the Bible that the Holy Spirit strives with men; speaks to men, and guides Christians. He calls and sends forth God's servants. Because he is God and sovereign, he cannot be persuaded or ordered to do or give anything to us.

The Holy Spirit in the Old Testament

Although the New Testament gives us the fuller revelation of the person and work of the Holy Spirit, the Old Testament is certainly not silent concerning his ministry. From the opening verses of the Bible, where it says the 'Spirit of God was hovering over the waters' (Gen.1:2), we are aware of the Spirit's existence in unison with the Father and the Son. As you read through the Old Testament you will see that the Holy Spirit came upon certain individuals and gave them unusual physical and spiritual ability. In the book of Judges we are told of Samson that 'the Spirit of the Lord came upon him in power. The ropes on his arms became like charred flax, and the bindings dropped from his hands' (Judges 15:14.). What is important to notice in the Old Testament is that such supernatural spiritual ability was not always linked with the individual's spirituality.

On at least three occasions in the Old Testament, God did promise to pour out his Spirit:

I will pour out my Spirit on your offspring and my blessing on your descendants' (Isaiah 44:3).

I will no longer hide my face from them, for I will pour out my Spirit on the house of Israel, declares the Sovereign Lord (Ezekiel 39:29).

I will pour out my Spirit on all people. Your sons and daughters will prophesy, your old men will dream dreams, and your young men will see visions. Even on my servants, both men and women. I will pour out my Spirit in those says' (Joel 2:28,29).

So the Old Testament is certainly not quiet concerning the person and work of the Holy Spirit.

.. and in the New Testament

Moving into the New Testament we find a fuller revelation of the work of the Holy Spirit right from the outset. The birth of our Saviour Jesus Christ was announced by an angel who came to Mary. His message was solemn and mysterious: 'The Holy Spirit will come upon you, and the power of the

Most High will overshadow you. So the holy one to be born will be called the Son of God' (Luke 1:35).

Zechariah, the father of John the Baptist, also received an angelic messenger who informed him that his son would be filled with the Holy Spirit even from birth' (Luke 1:15). Later on when Mary the mother of Jesus came to visit Elizabeth we are told that 'when Elizabeth heard Mary's greeting, the baby leaped in her womb, and Elizabeth was filled with the Holy Spirit' (Luke 1:41).

Clearly the two children were to be linked and as John the Baptist begins his public ministry he spoke of Jesus in conjunction with the work of the Holy Spirit: 'He will baptise you with the Holy Spirit and with fire' (Luke 3:16). At the baptism of Jesus, the Spirit demonstrates this link, working in these anointed cousins jointly: John recognised Jesus in the light of his saving and sacrificial purposes and Jesus is singled out by God through John as the Holy Spirit descended on him in bodily form like a dove (Luke 3:22).

Beginning his public ministry in Nazareth and reading the scroll of Isaiah in the synagogue, Jesus said, 'The Spirit of the Lord is on me because he has anointed me to preach ' (Luke 4:18) thus showing the Holy Spirit's involvement in his life and ministry which continued throughout his life. Jesus also spoke in his ministry, of a further coming of the Holy Spirit. The Spirit, he indicated, would come upon the believers acting as a comforter and reminder of all that Christ had done:

> The Counsellor, the Holy Spirit, whom the Father will send in my name, will teach you all things and will remind you of everything I have said to you (John 14:20).

> I will ask the Father, and he will give you another Counsellor to be with you for ever (John 14:16).

After his death and resurrection and before his ascension, Jesus gave to his disciples very precise instructions: 'Do not leave Jerusalem, but wait for the gift my Father promised, which you have heard me speak about' (Acts 1:4). They obeyed their Lord's command and after his ascension they gathered in an upper room in Jerusalem until the Day of Pentecost when the promise of Jesus was fulfilled (Acts 2).

Accompanying the gift of the Holy Spirit came the ability to speak in the languages of people from many parts of the world that were gathered in Jerusalem at that time. It was a unique and amazing event such as had never happened before or after. To try to seek for a repeat experience has no Biblical warrant.

How can I know the Holy Spirit?

Your first introduction to the Holy Spirit was when he began to convict you of your sin and your need to get right with God. Listening to God's Word as the gospel was preached, talking with a Christian friend, or reading a book, there was a distinct feeling of unease within. Sin, your sin, began to move from the area of a nebulous generality of all not being quite right to a more practical reality of knowing that you were a sinner. You felt a need to have your sin dealt with and to seek God's forgiveness.

At this point in your life you were beginning to experience the reality of what Jesus said was one of the great ministries of the Holy Spirit: 'When he comes, he will convict the world of guilt in regard to sin and righteousness and judgment' (John 16:8). After convicting you of sin, the Holy Spirit revealed to you Jesus (as he said he would) as the only Saviour of sinners: 'He will bring glory to me by taking from what is mine and making it known to you' (John 16:14). The Spirit pointed you to Christ and you saw that in him alone was forgiveness and salvation.

Then came that moment when you yielded to

Jesus Christ as he called you to him. The miracle brought you into God's family and you became a Christian. The Bible speaks of this as being 'born again', or being 'born of the Spirit'. This was the beginning of your personal relationship with the Holy Spirit. Now that it is established, it is a relationship that needs to grow and deepen throughout your life.

Paul reminds us that as well as this personal miracle of new birth in our lives, the Holy Spirit brings us into a fellowship: the church of Jesus Christ, or what the Bible speaks of as the 'body of Christ'. Writing to the Christians in Corinth Paul reminds them of an important truth concerning their relationship with the Holy Spirit: 'For we were all baptised by one Spirit into one body, whether Jews or Greeks, slave or free, and we were all given the one Spirit to drink' (1 Cor. 12:13).

You may meet some very sincere Christians who will tell you that you need to be 'baptized with the Holy Spirit' as a second experience, and that with that experience, you will be given the ability to speak in tongues. But that is not what the Scriptures teach. Ask yourself the question, 'When did I come into the body, the church?' Surely the answer is: when you were called to Christ and came to him. You were not a Christian first and then subsequently placed into the body of Christ, the church. At the moment of new birth you were baptized by the Spirit into Christ's body and placed in the church.

Even more revealing are these other words of Paul found in 1 Corinthians 6:19: 'Do you not know that your body is a temple of the Holy Spirit, who is in you, whom you have received from God? You are not your own.' The Holy Spirit has not only brought you into a relationship with God and a relationship with other Christians, but he has also come to take up residence in you. You are now a temple of God and you belong to him as much as he belongs to you.

The sealing of the Holy Spirit

God's gift of the Holy Spirit is also the seal that you belong to him.

He anointed us, set his seal of ownership on us, and put his Spirit in our hearts as a deposit guaranteeing what is to come' (2 Cor.1:21,22). Having believed, you were marked in him with a seal, the promised Holy Spirit, who is a deposit guaranteeing our inheritance' (Eph. 1: 13,14).

There are some who would suggest that this 'sealing of the Spirit' is an event totally distinct and subsequent to conversion. But this is certainly not the teaching of Scripture. There was no way in which Paul would have known personally all of those who had been converted in Ephesus, yet he refers to all of them when he says 'you were sealed.' If it was true of them, it is also true of you. It is important to remember that the seal is the Holy Spirit himself.

Now there are three things that a seal indicated and these can help us to understand our relationship with the Holy Spirit. First of all, it indicates *security.* A parallel use of the word meaning 'to seal' is found when the body of Jesus was taken down from the cross and put into a tomb. We are told the Jewish authorities, 'went and made the tomb secure by putting a seal on the stone' (Matt. 27:66).

Secondly, a seal speaks of *ownership,* and the Ephesians would certainly have understood this picture. Ephesus was a port with an extensive trade in timber. After selecting timber, local merchants stamped it with their own signet ring and this was recognised as the sign of ownership. Very often they did not immediately carry off the timber they had bought, but it was left in the harbour with all the other logs. But the important thing was that it had been chosen, paid for, and stamped. Later the merchant would send an agent with the signet ring and he looked for the corresponding image on the timber, claimed it and took it away. God's gift to you of his Holy Spirit is his sign that you are divinely owned, that you belong to him.

Sealing is also a mark of *recognition*. Writing to Timothy Paul says, 'God's solid foundation stands firm, sealed with this inscription: The Lord knows those who are his' (2 Tim. 2:19). God does not look upon us as a mass, but rather as individuals. God's gift of the Holy Spirit to you means that you are safe and secure, that he knows you by name, and that you belong to him.

The ongoing work of the Spirit

But this is not the end of the work of the Holy Spirit on your behalf. Rather it is the beginning, for there is a continuing work of the Spirit that we should enjoy day by day: 'Because you are sons, God sent the Spirit of his Son into our hearts, the Spirit who calls out, "Abba, Father"' (Gal.4:6). 'The natural man,' says Paul, 'does not receive the things of God.' But the 'spiritual man', the man born again, has inside information. God's Spirit speaking to you through the Word of God will give you an increasing spiritual understanding limited in no way by your intellectual abilities.

Jesus also teaches us that the ministry of the

Holy Spirit is to glorify him. 'He will bring glory to me by taking from what is mine and making it known to you' (John 16:14). In addition, it is the work of the Holy Spirit to set us free:

Therefore, there is now no condemnation for those who are in Christ Jesus, because through Christ Jesus, the law of the Spirit of life set me free from the law of sin and death (Rom.8:1,2).

His power for service

One attribute of the Holy Spirit that is very clear from the New Testament is this: the Holy Spirit is the Spirit of power to enable believers to witness: 'But you will receive power when the Holy Spirit comes on you' (Acts 1:8). As you read through the Acts of the Apostles you will discover that you are reading the activities of the Spirit in and through the apostles and other believers.

Let's look at some of them: in Acts 2:4, we read of the disciples being 'filled with the Spirit'. Of Stephen we read: 'But Stephen, full of the Holy Spirit, looked up to heaven and saw the glory of God, and Jesus standing at the right hand of God' (7:55). Philip, one of the seven chosen in Acts 6 to 'wait at tables,' became the great evangelist to Samaria. When Paul and Barnabas were in the church in Antioch, it was the Holy Spirit who said,

'Set apart for me Barnabas and Saul for the work to which I have called them' (Acts 13:2). And the reason why those early disciples had power, wisdom, boldness, steadfastness, evangelistic zeal and missionary enterprise, was because they were all filled with the Holy Spirit.

His power to sanctify

The word 'sanctify' has a number of uses in the Bible. It is used, for example, of the putting aside of certain things for a holy purpose and for God's exclusive use. Moses uses the term in this way in Leviticus 27:14 when he speaks of a man 'dedicating his house (or sanctifying it) to the Lord.'

Peter urges you as a Christian to 'in your heart set apart Christ as Lord' (1 Peter 3:15). But in the New Testament the word 'sanctify' or 'set apart' also means 'to make holy by cleansing from sin.' 'From the beginning God chose you to be saved through the sanctifying work of the Spirit' (2 Thess.2:13). Sanctification means being set apart from all that spoils our walk with God, and being dedicated to him, with a subsequent growth in holiness and godly living. The topics or subjects covered in this book are therefore all part of this sanctifying process. Because of that we can be encouraged that we have the help of the Holy Spirit in achieving these aims for a healthy, holy Christian life.

Let me remind you what I stressed at the beginning of this chapter: the Holy Spirit is a person, and as a person he cannot be divided. You cannot have a part of him, because that would be impossible. But the question is, does he have all of you? The Holy Spirit having all of you is what sanctification is all about.

Your righteousness is Christ *for* you, but your sanctification is Christ *in* you. Sanctification is not so much what he does, but what he is himself within you by the Holy Spirit. The work of the Spirit within you is not to help you to imitate Christ, for that is an impossible goal; but rather his work within you is to reproduce Christ. It is also important in this connection to realise that his work is not to eradicate the old nature that you still have even after you have become a Christian but rather to counteract it. Paul says:

Live by the Spirit, and you will not gratify the desires of the sinful nature' (Gal.5:16).
Through Christ Jesus the law of the Spirit of life set me free from the law of sin and death' (Rom.8:2).

If, unable to swim, you were to fall into a deep lake, you would sink and drown because of the law of gravity. But if someone threw you a life belt and you placed it round your waist then you would float. A higher law had come into play. It had not eradicated the law of gravitation, but it had counteracted it. It is this higher law of the 'Spirit of life' that can counteract the desires and works of your old nature and lift you above them. Because Christ lives in us, what we cannot copy, the Holy Spirit can reproduce; what we cannot eradicate, he can neutralise by his counteracting power.

God has not removed your old nature and brought you into a position where it is impossible to sin, but he has imparted to you the divine nature and given you his Holy Spirit so that you are now able to live a holy life. This is the ongoing work of sanctification in you by the Holy Spirit. So now the question to consider is: how does the Holy Spirit, who lives and dwells in your life, accomplish your sanctification?

Firstly, the Holy Spirit is *the great revealer*. We already noted this when we were thinking earlier of how important it was to recognise that he is a person and not just an influence. Jesus said, in John 16:15, to his disciples, 'All that belongs to the Father is mine. That is why I said the Spirit will take from what is mine and make it known to you.'

As the Holy Spirit reveals to us the beauty and

the holiness of the Lord Jesus Christ we are bound to see just how far short we have come of what he requires from us. We begin to see in the light of his radiance our own inconsistencies, our short-comings and sin. We can be sure of this: the Holy Spirit will always show us what is wrong, but never just to leave us despondent. He will also show us the way of cleansing, forgiveness and renewal. Paul says, 'Since we live by the Spirit, let us keep in step with the Spirit' (Gal.5:25). The phrase, 'keep in step' is a very interesting one and simply means, 'proceed, step in order, follow the pattern.' So where is the pattern? It is in God's Word, the Bible. Obedience to God's revealed will in his Word means that you are walking in the Spirit.

Someone has said that a pilgrimage of a thou-sand miles begins with a single step. So it is with spiritual growth. It is not achieved once for all, in an instantaneous event; rather it is a progres-sive lifelong pursuit. Walking involves time and persistence, it needs initiative and purpose.

The Holy Spirit is also *the great remover.* Christians live in an evil, sinful world and there-fore cannot help coming into contact with evil. But we must rely upon the Holy Spirit to help us renounce it and be separate from it in every way. Paul said, 'Do not grieve the Holy Spirit of God, with whom you were sealed for the day of redemption' (Eph.4:30). Anything that we allow in our lives that is unholy or displeasing to God will grieve him, because holiness is an intrinsic part of his person.

Grieving him by sinning will rebound on us, because it is the Holy Spirit who ministers Christ to us and through us. He is the one who pours in the balm of God's grace and peace into our lives. Paul emphasises this truth when writing to the Thessalonian Christians: 'Do not put out the Spirit's fire' (1 Thess.5:19); and to the believers in Corinth he writes: 'Let us purify ourselves from everything that contaminates body and spirit, perfecting holiness out of reverence for God' (2 Cor. 7:1).

God cannot bless those who compromise with evil. We must be determined day by day that although we cannot completely separate ourselves from contact with evil, we can make sure that we do not conform to it and so grieve the Holy Spirit.

We must be careful also not to grieve the Holy Spirit for the sake of others. God touches lives through our lives. People will hear the gospel and meet the gospel through us, so it is very important that we don't hinder their understanding of the gospel by what we allow in our lives. The Holy Spirit needs a clean channel through which he can flow in blessing to others.

It is as we respond to his revealing and convicting presence that he will impart to us God's power to separate from anything that comes between us and our Lord. Paul reminds us of this great responsibility and opportunity:

I pray that out of his glorious riches he may strengthen you with power through his Spirit in your inner being, so that Christ may dwell in your hearts through faith' (Eph.3:16,17).

And we pray this in order that you may live a life worthy of the Lord and may please him in every way: bearing fruit in every good work, growing in the knowledge of God, being strengthened with all power according to his glorious might' (Col.1:10,11).

All of God's resources are available to us when we are indwelt by the Spirit, and his grace is sufficient to enable us to renounce every evil thing he discovers in us. In addition, the Spirit within will also increasingly take away even the desire for them and create in their place a lovely desire for the opposite as you yield to him and follow his promptings. So whatever the temptation is that you may face, the antidote to it is the Spirit within. Frederick Wood, the founder of the National Young Life Campaign described this power as 'the expulsive power of a new affection.'

Thirdly, the Holy Spirit is *the great renewer.* Writing to the Roman Christians Paul said, 'Do not conform any longer to the pattern of this world, but be transformed by the renewing of your mind' (Rom.12:2.). Growth always takes time, and the Holy Spirit as the great renewer takes time to change us. He takes away what is unlike the Lord Jesus and he transforms us into the image of Christ. He has to burn out the dross of sin and brand us with the pattern of Christ, and this does not happen overnight. In this age of the instant, do not be deceived into thinking that there is a short cut to holiness and sanctification. It is going to be an ongoing process from now until you are finally ushered into the presence of the Lord at the end of your life.

Paul, in Ephesians 5:18 says, 'Do not get drunk on wine, which leads to debauchery, instead be filled with the Spirit' or a more accurate translation would be 'be being filled with the Spirit.' It is an interesting picture that Paul uses here as he describes the difference between being drunk on wine and being filled with the Holy Spirit. A drunkard wants to get more of the drink, but for a Christian it is not just getting more of the Holy Spirit, but rather him getting more of us.

A drunkard often has by an immense feeling of

well being, and so should a Spirit-filled Christian. A drunkard is recognised by his speech and manner of walking: a Spirit-filled believer should by talk and way of life give clear evidence that God is within him.

So if you 'walk in the Spirit', being very careful not to 'grieve the spirit' and also day by day seek to be 'filled with the Spirit,' then you will not only grow but he will gift you in some way or ways in order that you might serve God. Paul writing to the Galatian Christians after first of all challenging them to 'live by the Spirit,' so that they do not gratify the desires of the flesh, then goes on to outline what the positive fruit of the Spirit should be in their lives:

> But the fruit of the Spirit is love, joy, peace, patience, kindness, goodness, faithfulness, gentleness and self control. Against such things there is no law ... Since we live by the Spirit, let us keep in step with the Spirit' (Gal.5:22-25).

What a contrast this is to the previous verses where Paul speaks of the 'acts of the sinful nature' (Gal. 5:19). Actions have their source in self whereas fruit originates from the Spirit. Action declare what a person does, but fruit manifests what a person is. Actions show conduct, but fruit reveals character. In actions the emphasis is on doing, but in fruit the stress is on being.

Will you also notice that it is the 'fruit of the Spirit' and not fruits? The fruit, however, does have a nine-fold expression. If you are walking in the Spirit then he will produce all of these nine qualities in your life.

Jesus said to his disciples, 'I am the vine; you are the branches. If a man remains in me and I in him, he will bear much fruit; apart from me you can do nothing' (John 15:5). The source of this fruit is not therefore in you but in Christ himself. The indwelling Holy Spirit works in you to produce the character of Christ.

As you respond to his inner promptings and follow his leading you will find yourself growing and branching out as a Christian. The Holy Spirit is the key to that growth as he guides you through God's handbook, the Bible. In his power and under his instruction the topics we have covered in this book will be opened up to you. If you keep in step with the Spirit, he will continually point you to Christ into whose likeness you will steadily grow. In this way, you will be found among those who 'grow in grace and in the knowledge of our Lord Jesus Christ'.

That's what Christian growth is all about.